first time
SEWING

First published in 2014 by Creative Publishing international, an imprint of The Quarto Group,
100 Cummings Center, Suite 265-D, Beverly, MA 01915, USA.
T (978) 282-9590 F (978) 283-2742 QuartoKnows.com

Creative Publishing international titles are also available at discount for retail, wholesale, promotional, and bulk purchase. For details, contact the Special Sales Manager by email at specialsales@quarto.com or by mail at The Quarto Group, Attn: Special Sales Manager, 100 Cummings Center, Suite 265-D, Beverly, MA 01915, USA.

ISBN: 978-1-58923-804-6

18

Digital edition published in 2014
eISBN: 978-1-62788-009-1

Library of Congress Cataloging-in-Publication Data available

Cover Design, Book Design, and Page Layout: Megan Jones Design
Illustrations: Heather Lambert
Front cover photo: Shutterstock.com

Printed in China

first time

SEWING

THE ABSOLUTE BEGINNER'S GUIDE

by the editors of Creative Publishing international

Creative Publishing
international

contents

introduction

WELCOME TO THE CREATIVE, REWARDING WORLD OF SEWING. *FIRST TIME SEWING* IS DESIGNED TO MAKE YOUR LEARNING EXPERIENCE AS PAINLESS AS POSSIBLE AND TO INSTILL CONFIDENCE AS YOU TAKE ON NEW PROJECTS AND LEARN NEW TECHNIQUES. EASY-TO-FOLLOW INSTRUCTIONS WITH COLORFUL PHOTOGRAPHS HELP YOU BUILD YOUR SEWING SKILLS WHILE MAKING CLOTHES, GIFTS, AND HOME DECORATING ITEMS YOU'LL BE PLEASED TO USE, SHARE, AND WEAR.

Sewing enthusiasts enjoy this time-honored art for many reasons. Sewing your own clothes still gives you the advantage of personalized fit and individual expression. Home decorating items are popular projects for beginners and advanced sewers alike, partly because of the cost savings over purchased items. By sewing these items for the home, you also get to enjoy the creative fun of choosing styles, colors, and fabrics that fit your personality and taste. But perhaps the greatest reason that sewing is so enjoyable is the mere satisfaction felt in creating something from scratch with your own two hands. Whether you are making something for yourself, your home, or to give to someone else, the ultimate reward is the intangible delight and personal fulfillment gained in the process.

The projects in this book are designed to guide you from your first nervous stitch at your sewing machine to comfortable familiarity. Each project will teach you new skills. Throughout the book you will find tips to make your sewing easier or more efficient and explanations to help you understand the reasons behind the methods.

Use the first section of the book to acquaint yourself with your sewing machine and the techniques and supplies that encompass the art of sewing. Your sewing machine owner's manual is a necessity; refer to it first if you have questions or problems specific to your machine. The first step in any sewing project is to read through the directions from beginning to end. Refer to the Tell Me More sidebars for definitions or elaborations on bold key words or phrases used in the project. At the beginning of every project you will find a list of the necessary materials. Read through the information on fabrics before you go shopping, so the fabric store will seem a little more user-friendly when you get there. Above all, enjoy the process. Give yourself the opportunity to be creative, and express yourself through the things you sew.

SEWING BASICS

There is no better place to start than at the very beginning. If you are starting from scratch, even a trip to the fabric store can be challenging. Manufacturers can't include all the vital information with their packaging, and there are so many tools and sewing notions to choose from. To give you a firm foundation for learning to sew, this section teaches you the essentials about your sewing machine, fabrics, patterns, and sewing supplies. If you have never taken a stitch, you will appreciate the detailed information, photos, and illustrations. Even if you have a little sewing experience, you are sure to learn some things you didn't know. So settle back, take your time, and jump into the basics.

the sewing machine

The principle parts common to all modern sewing machines are shown in the diagram at right. The parts may look different on your model, and they may have slightly different locations, so open your owner's manual, also. If you do not have an owner's manual for your machine, contact a sewing machine dealer who sells your brand or search the Internet. Become familiar with the names of the parts and their functions. As you spend more time sewing, these items will become second nature to you.

If you are buying a new machine, consider how much and what kind of sewing you expect to do. Talk to friends who sew and to sales personnel. Ask for demonstrations, and sew on the machine yourself. Experiment with the various features while sewing on a variety of fabrics, including knits, wovens, lightweights, and denim. Think about the optional features of the machine and which ones you want on yours. Many dealers offer free sewing lessons with the purchase of a machine. Take advantage! These lessons will be geared to your particular brand and model of sewing machine.

These parts are common to all sewing machines, but their position and design differs. Use your manual to help you learn where these parts are, what these parts do, and how to use them:

Bobbin

Bobbin case

Bobbin winder spindle

Bobbin winder tension

Buttonhole knob

Detachable machine bed

Food dogs

Feed dog control

General-purpose presser foot

Handwheel

Light switch

Needle clamp

Presser foot lifter

Presser foot pressure control

Seam allowance guide

Spool pins

Stitch pattern selector

Stitch length selector

Stitch width selector

Take-up lever

Top tension control

Top tension discs

Thread cutter

Thread guides

Throat plate

Variable speed switch

machine accessories

SEWING MACHINE NEEDLES

Sewing machine needles come in a variety of styles and sizes. The correct needle choice depends mostly on the fabric you have selected. Sharp points (A), used for woven fabrics, are designed to pierce the fabric. Ballpoints (B) are designed to slip between the loops of knit fabric rather than pierce and possibly damage the fabric. Universal points are designed to work on both woven and knitted fabrics. The size of the needle is designated by a number, generally given in both American (9, 11, 12, 14, 16, 18) and European (60, 70, 80, 90, 100, 110) numbering systems. Use size 11/70 or 12/80 needles for mediumweight fabrics. A larger number means the needle is thicker and that it is appropriate for use with heavier fabrics and heavier threads.

BOBBINS

Stitches are made by locking the upper thread with a lower thread, carried on a bobbin. Always use bobbins in the correct style and size for your machine. Bobbin thread tension is controlled by a spring on the bobbin case, which may be built in (C) or removable (D).

A

B

 TIP *Though needle style and size are usually indicated in some way on the needle, it is often difficult to see without a magnifying glass, and you most likely will not remember what needle is in the machine. As an easy reminder, when you finish a sewing session, leave a fabric swatch from your current project under the presser foot.*

PRESSER FEET

Every sewing machine comes with accessories for specialized tasks. More can be purchased as you develop your interest and skills. Your machine manual or dealer can show you what accessories are available and will explain how to use them to get the best results.

A

A general-purpose foot (A), probably the one you will use most often, has a wide opening to accommodate the side-to-side movement of the needle in all types of utility (nondecorative) stitches. It is also suitable for most straight stitching. A zipper foot (B) is used to insert zippers or to stitch any seam that has more bulk on one side than the other. For some sewing machines, the zipper foot is stationary, requiring you to move the needle position to the right or left. For other styles, the position of the zipper foot itself is adjustable. A special-purpose or embroidery foot (C) has a grooved bottom that allows the foot to ride smoothly over decorative stitches or raised cords. Some styles are clear plastic, allowing you to see your work more clearly. A walking foot (D) feeds top and bottom layers at equal rates, allowing you to more easily match patterns or stitch bulky layers as for quilting.

B

C

D

sewing supplies

Sewing involves many steps: measuring, laying out the pattern, cutting, marking, stitching, and pressing. For each of these steps there are special tools and supplies to make your sewing easier and help you complete your projects successfully. Don't feel you need to buy all the items before you start. For instance, a pair of sharp shears and a seam ripper will see you through most of the cutting tasks for the projects in this book. You will undoubtedly acquire additional tools as your skills and interests grow.

HAND-SEWING SUPPLIES

Needles and pins are available in a variety of sizes and styles. Look for rustproof needles and pins made of brass, nickel-plated steel, or stainless steel. Pictured from top to bottom:

Sharps are all-purpose, medium-length needles designed for general sewing.

Crewels are sharp, large-eyed medium-length needles, designed for embroidery.

Betweens are very short and round-eyed. They are useful for hand quilting and making fine stitches.

Milliner's needles are long with round eyes and are used for making long basting or gathering stitches.

Pins with colored ball heads are easier to see and are less likely to get lost than those with flat heads.

Straight pins are used for general sewing. They should be slim and are usually 1¹⁄₁₆" (2.7 cm) long.

Quilting pins are 1¾" (4.5 cm) long. Their extra length makes them ideal for use on bulky fabrics or fabrics with extra loft.

A A **thimble** protects your finger while hand sewing. Available in a variety of styles and sizes, it is worn on whichever finger you use to push the needle through the fabric. Most people prefer either the middle or ring finger. Using a thimble is an acquired habit. Some people can't get along without one, while others feel they are a nuisance.

B **Pincushions** provide a safe and handy place to store pins. One style is worn on the wrist for convenience. Another style, a magnetic tray, attracts and holds steel pins. Be careful not to place any magnetic tools near a computerized machine, because the magnet may interfere with the machine's memory.

C **Needle threaders** ease threading of hand and machine needles. This is especially useful if you have difficulty seeing something that small.

D Thread can be drawn through **beeswax** to strengthen it and prevent it from tangling while hand sewing.

MEASURING & MARKING TOOLS

A **Transparent ruler** allows you to see what you are measuring and marking. It also is used to check fabric grainline.

B **Yardstick** (meterstick) should be made of smooth hardwood or metal.

C **Tape measure** has the flexibility helpful for measuring items with shape and dimension. Select one made of a material that will not stretch.

D **Seam gauge** is a 6" (15 cm) metal or plastic ruler with a sliding marker. It helps take quick, accurate measurements and can be used to measure seam allowance widths.

E **Transparent T-square** is used to locate grainline and to measure 90-degree angles.

F **Marking chalk** is available in several forms: as powder in a rolling wheel dispenser, as a pencil, or as a flat slice. Chalk lines are easily removable from most fabrics.

G **Fabric marking pens** are available in both air-erasable and water-erasable forms. Air-erasable marks disappear within 48 hours; water-erasable marks wash off with a sprinkling of water.

H **Narrow masking tape** is an alternative method for marking fabrics when other methods are less suitable.

CUTTING TOOLS

Buy quality cutting tools and use them only for your sewing! Cutting paper or other household materials will dull your cutting tools quickly. Dull tools are not only tiresome to work with, they can also damage fabric. Scissors have both handles the same size; shears have one handle larger than the other. Have your cutting tools sharpened periodically by a qualified professional.

Bent-handled dressmaker's shears are best for cutting out project pieces because the angle of the lower blade lets fabric lie flat on the cutting surface. Blade lengths of 7" or 8" (18 or 20.5 cm) are most popular, but lengths of up to 12" (30.5 cm) are available. Select a blade length appropriate for the size of your hand; shorter lengths for smaller hands. Left-handed models are also available.

Sewing scissors with pointed tips are handy for clipping threads and trimming and clipping seam allowances. A 6" (15 cm) blade is suitable for most tasks.

Seam ripper quickly removes stitches and opens buttonholes. Use it carefully to avoid cutting the fabric.

Rotary cutter works like a pizza cutter and can be used by left-handed or right-handed sewers. A locking mechanism retracts the blade for safety. Use the rotary cutter with a special plastic mat, available in different sizes, with or without gridlines. The self-healing mat protects both the work surface and the blade.

Pinking shears and pinking rotary cutters are used to finish seam allowances. They cut fabric in a zigzag or scalloped pattern instead of a straight line.

PRESSING TOOLS

Pressing at each stage of construction is the secret to a perfectly finished garment. The general rule is to press each stitched seam before crossing it with another.

A **Steam/spray iron** should have a wide temperature range to accommodate all fabrics. Buy a dependable, name-brand iron. An iron that steams and sprays at any setting, not just the higher heat settings, is helpful for fabrics with synthetic fibers.

B **Press cloth** helps prevent iron shine and is always used when applying fusibles. The transparent cloth allows you to see if the fabric is smooth and the layers are properly aligned.

C **Teflon-coated sole plate guard**, available to fit most irons, eliminates the need for a press cloth.

D **Seam roll** is a firmly packed cylindrical cushion for pressing seams. The bulk of the fabric falls to the sides away from the iron, preventing the seam from making an imprint on the right side of the fabric.

E **Pressing ham** is a firmly packed cushion for pressing curved areas of a garment.

F **Sleeve board** looks like two small ironing boards attached one on top of the other. It is useful for pressing sleeves one layer at a time to avoid unwanted creases.

special products

Many special products and gadgets are designed to assist you in various steps of the sewing process. Before using a new product, read the manufacturer's instructions carefully. Learn what special handling or care is required, and for what fabrics or sewing techniques it is especially suited. Here are some specialized products that you may find helpful in sewing your clothes, accessories, or home décor items.

A **Cutting boards** protect table finishes from scratches. Available in cardboard, plastic, or padded styles, these boards also hold fabric more securely while cutting. Square off fabric using the marked lines, and use the 1" (2.5 cm) squares as an instant measure.

B **Elastics** can be purchased in a variety of widths and styles, either in precut lengths or by the yard (meter). Softer elastics (a) are suitable for pajamas or boxer shorts; nonroll elastic (b) stays flat in the casing; some wide elastic has channels for topstitching (c).

C **Interfacing** plays a supporting role in almost every garment. It is an inner layer of fabric, used to stabilize the fabric in areas like necklines and waistbands, or give support behind buttons and buttonholes. Interfacings may be woven, nonwoven, or knit; the easiest forms to use are heat fusible and these should come with instructions.

D A **bodkin** is used to thread elastic or cording through a casing. One end holds the elastic tightly while you feed the tool through the narrow casing, pulling the elastic or cording behind it.

(continued)

E **Point turner** is helpful for perfecting corners, such as at the top of a pocket or at the ends of a waistband, or inside a pillow cover. Slip the tool inside the item, and gently poke the fabric out into a point.

F **Liquid fray preventer** is a colorless plastic liquid that prevents fraying by stiffening the fabric slightly. It is helpful when you have clipped too far into a seam allowance or want to reinforce a buttonhole. It may discolor some fabrics, so test before using, and apply carefully. The liquid may be removed with rubbing alcohol. It dries to a permanent finish that will withstand laundering and dry cleaning.

G **Glue stick** is a convenient substitute for pinning or basting when you need to hold an item in place temporarily before stitching. The temporary adhesive in a retractable tube can be applied in small dots. It won't discolor the fabric and washes out completely, if necessary. It will not harm your machine or gum up your needle as you stitch through it.

H **Buttonhole cutter** is a handy tool for making precision cuts down the center of buttonholes. It comes with a wooden block to place under the fabric to protect your work surface and accept the sharp thin blade of the cutter. While buttonholes can be cut open with small scissors or a seam ripper, a buttonhole cutter is more accurate and less likely to cut the stitches.

Basting tape is double-faced adhesive tape used instead of pinning or basting. It is especially helpful for matching prints, applying zippers, and positioning trims. Some manufacturers advise that you avoid stitching through the tape because the adhesive may collect on your needle.

Single-fold bias tape is useful for hemming curved edges, such as a round tablecloth. The manufacturer has already cut the bias strips, sewn them together, and pressed in precise folds to make your sewing easier. The tape is available in packaged lengths in a wide ranges of colors.

Paper-backed fusible web is sold on rolls, in various narrow widths. It is also available as a wide sheet rolled on a bolt for purchase by the yard (meter). It is a time-saving product used for adhering two pieces of fabric together. For instance, you may use narrow strips of it to secure the side hems of a Roman shade instead of stitching them. A protective paper backing is removed from one side after the other side has been fused to the fabric.

Blanket binding resembles a wide satin ribbon that has been pressed in half for encasing the raw edge around a blanket. Packaged in a convenient length for sewing baby blankets, the binding is available in assorted soft colors and white. Because of its stability and permanent crease, it is easy to work with, yet feels silky smooth against a baby's skin.

fabric information

Selecting the right fabrics for your projects may seem like an overwhelming task, but there are a few simple guidelines to help narrow the field. One good way to learn about fabrics is to browse through a fabric store, handling the fabrics and reading the fiber content information and care instructions printed on the ends of the bolts. You may already know whether you want a solid color, a printed pattern, or perhaps a multicolored fabric. Do you need a fabric that can be laundered frequently? Do you want smooth or textured, stiff or drapable, lightweight or heavy? Some basic fabric knowledge and a thought-out plan will help you make wise choices and avoid costly errors.

FIBER CONTENT

Natural fabrics are made from plant or animal fibers, spun into yarns: cotton, wool, silk, and linen are most common. Naturals are often considered the easiest fabrics to sew. Synthetic fabrics, made from chemically produced fibers, include nylon, acrylic, acetate, and polyester. Rayon is a man-made fiber made from a plant source. Each fiber has unique characteristics, desirable for different reasons. Many fabrics are a blend of natural and synthetic fibers, offering you the best qualities of each, such as the breathable comfort of cotton blended with the wrinkle resistance of polyester.

WOVEN FABRICS

Woven fabrics have straight lengthwise and crosswise yarns. The pattern in which the yarns are woven gives the fabric its characteristic surface texture and appearance. The outer edges of woven fabrics are called selvages. As a general rule, they should be trimmed away because they are often heavier than the rest of the fabric, and they may shrink when laundered or pressed. Grainlines are the directions in which the fabric yarns run. Strong, stable lengthwise yarns, running parallel to the selvages, form the lengthwise grain. The crosswise grain is perpendicular to the lengthwise grain and has a small amount of give. Any diagonal direction, called the bias, has a fair amount of stretch.

KNIT FABRICS

Knit fabrics consist of rows of interlocking loops of yarn, as in a hand-knit sweater, but usually on a finer scale. Knit fabrics are more flexible than other fabrics, and they all stretch. These features mean that garments made of knits require less fitting and offer more freedom of movement. When sewing with knits, select patterns that are specifically designed for knit fabrics.

Knit fabric is made from interlocking looped stitches. The lengthwise rows of stitches are called ribs; the crosswise rows are called courses. These ribs and courses correspond to the lengthwise and crosswise grains of woven fabrics.

Patterns designed for knit fabrics have a stretch gauge. Fold over the fabric along a crosswise course several inches (centimeters) from a cut end, and test its degree of stretch against the gauge. If the fabric stretches the necessary amount without distortion, it is suitable for the pattern.

Stretch terry

Synthetic fleece

Double knit

Sweatshirt fleece

Novelty knit

DECORATOR FABRICS

Moiré

Twill weave

Cotton sateen print

Jacquard

Cotton sateen

Novelty weave

FABRIC SHOPPING

Fabrics in a store are divided into fashion fabrics and decorator fabrics. Decorator fabrics are generally more durable than fashion fabrics; most have stain-resistant finishes. They are designed for pillows, slipcovers, window treatments, and other home decorating projects. They are manufactured in widths (crosswise grain) of 48" or 54" (122 or 137 cm), though occasionally you may find some wider. To prevent creases, decorator fabrics are rolled on tubes.

Fashion fabrics are usually folded double and rolled on cardboard bolts. They vary in width; the most common are 36", 45", and 60" (91.5, 115, and 152.5 cm). Though fashion fabrics are intended for apparel, many of them are also suitable for home decorating. Most stores arrange their fashion fabrics according to the fiber content or fabric style. For example, all the wools and wool blends, suitable for skirts, slacks, and jackets, may be found together in one area of the store; all the bridal and special-occasion fabrics located in another area; quilting fabrics (lightweight cottons) in another. This is not a hard-and-fast rule, however, so you will want to spend time getting acquainted with the fabric stores you shop.

FABRIC PREPARATION

Preshrink washable fabric before cutting out the project, by washing and drying it in the same way you will care for the finished item. Because most decorator fabrics are not washable and require dry cleaning when necessary, preshrink them by pressing with steam, moving the iron evenly along the grainlines. Allow the fabric to dry before moving it.

FASHION FABRICS

Cotton corduroy

Silk

Polyester fleece

Cotton denim

Linen

selecting a pattern

Major pattern companies follow a uniform sizing based on standard body measurements. This is not exactly the same as ready-to-wear sizing.

DETERMINING SIZE

To select the right pattern size, first take your standard body measurements. Wear your usual undergarments and use a tape measure that doesn't stretch. It may be easier to have another person measure you. Record your measurements and compare them with the size chart on the back of the pattern or in the pattern book.

TAKING STANDARD BODY MEASUREMENTS

1 Waistline. Tie a string or piece of elastic around your middle, and allow it to roll to your natural waistline. Measure at this exact location with a tape measure. Leave the string in place as a reference for measuring your hips and back waist length.

2 Hips. Measure around the fullest part of your hips. This is usually 7" to 9" (18 to 23 cm) below the waistline, depending on your height.

3 Bust. Place the tape measure under your arms, across the widest part of the back and the fullest part of the bustline.

4 Back waist length. Measure from the middle of the most prominent bone at the base of the neck down to the waistline string.

PATTERN SELECTION

Selecting a pattern for a garment allows for more creativity than shopping from a ready-to-wear catalog. Pattern catalogs don't limit you to certain fabric, colors, skirt lengths, or types of trims shown on the pages. You are free to choose a combination of features that best reflect your style and are most flattering to you.

Major pattern companies publish new catalogs with each season, which means that designer trends seen in clothing stores are reflected in the newest pattern catalogs along with more classic styles. You'll find simple patterns for sewers who prefer the quick and easy styles, and more detailed patterns for experienced sewers. The number of pattern pieces listed on the back of the pattern will provide a clue to the complexity of the pattern. The fewer pieces, the easier the project. Also, the pattern may indicate whether it is intended for knits only.

Pattern catalogs are usually divided into categories by garment types and marked by index tabs. The newest fashions often appear in the first few pages of each category. Pattern illustrations are accompanied by information on recommended fabrics and yardage requirements. An index at the back of the catalog lists patterns in numerical order along with their page numbers. The back of the catalog also includes a complete size chart for every figure type.

all about patterns

The pattern envelope is a selling tool and an educational device. The front generally has a photograph of the finished garment and several drawings of the variations that can be sewn using the pattern. On the pattern back, you'll find detailed information to help you select fabric and all the notions necessary to complete your project.

THE ENVELOPE FRONT

Pattern company name, and style number that corresponds to the number in the catalog, are displayed prominently.

Size or sizes included in the pattern are indicated near the number. Most patterns include several sizes.

Photograph or fashion illustration shows the main pattern design made up in suitable fabrics. It also indicates how closely or loosely the pattern is intended to fit.

Labels may indicate special considerations: that a pattern is suitable for knits only, is easy to sew, has special fitting or size-related information.

Views, labeled with letters, are alternate designs that can be sewn using the pattern. They may include variations in length, fullness, or other design details.

THE ENVELOPE BACK

Fabric amounts required for each view in all the available sizes are listed in a chart. Locate the style view and the fabric width at the left; match it with your size at the top. The number where the two columns meet is the amount of fabric you need to buy. Interfacing and elastic requirements are also listed. Metric equivalents are given in a separate chart.

Fabrics recommended for sewing the garments are listed to help you make your selections. This paragraph will also tell you if certain fabrics are unsuitable, such as stripes or one way designs.

Number of pattern pieces gives you an idea of how easy or complicated the pattern is to sew.

Style number is repeated on the pattern back.

Notions, such as thread, buttons, and zippers, are listed in another paragraph.

Descriptions of the garment include its style, how it is intended to fit, and construction information for each of the views.

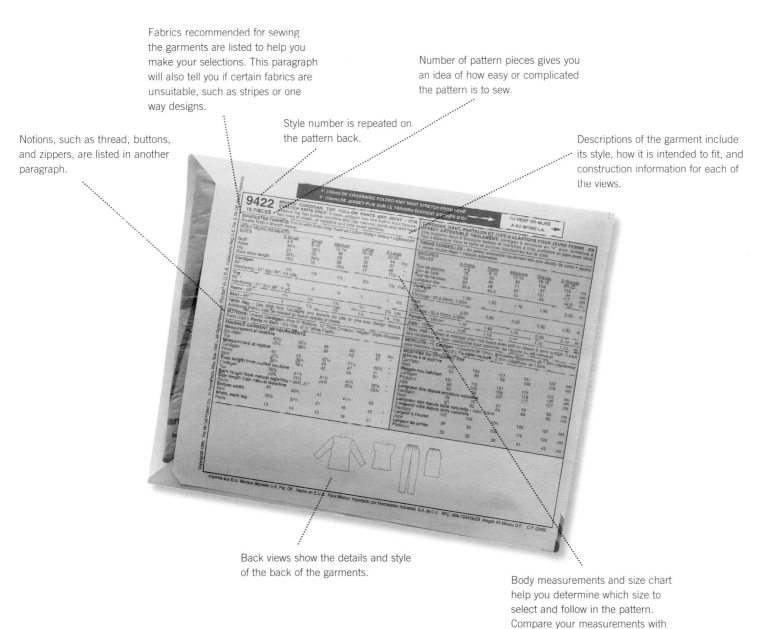

Back views show the details and style of the back of the garments.

Body measurements and size chart help you determine which size to select and follow in the pattern. Compare your measurements with those in the chart.

inside the pattern

Even if you love a good puzzle, your first peek at the pattern innards can be scary. Here's what to expect.

PATTERN FEATURES

Detailed sketches show you both front and back of each view.

General sewing directions, given as a short refresher course, include a key to the symbols used on the pattern pieces, and some basic construction techniques.

Cutting layouts for different fabric widths are shown for each view, in every size. Alternative layouts are shown for fabric with or without nap.

Pattern key, identifying every pattern piece by name and number.

Sewing directions are a step-by-step guide through the construction of the garment. Each step is accompanied by a sketch. The right side of the fabric usually appears shaded; the wrong side is plain. Interfacing is often indicated with dots.

pattern layout

All pattern companies use a universal system of symbols on their pattern pieces. These symbols help you lay out the pattern, show you where to cut, help you match up seamlines, show you where to sew, and give placement guides for things like buttons, buttonholes, and hems. Along with the symbols, you will also find essential instructions printed on the pattern pieces.

FOLDLINE. Often indicated by a long bracket with arrows at each end, it may have "place on fold" instructions. Place the pattern piece with the fold-line exactly on the fold of the fabric.

DOTS (large and small), squares, or triangles found along the seamlines indicate areas of construction where precise matching, clipping, or stitching is essential.

GRAINLINE. Heavy solid line with arrows at each end. Place the pattern piece on the fabric with the grainline running parallel to the selvage.

ADJUSTMENT LINE. Double line indicating where the pattern can be lengthened or shortened before cutting out the fabric. If an alteration is necessary, cut the pattern on the double line; spread evenly to lengthen, or overlap evenly to shorten.

CUTTING LINE. Heavy solid line along the outer edge of the pattern, often shown with a scissors symbol. Cut on this line. When more than one size is printed on one pattern, the cutting lines may be various styles of solid, dotted, or dashed lines, to help you distinguish one size from the next.

SEAMLINES. Long, broken line, usually ⅝" (1.5 cm) inside the cutting line. Multisize patterns often do not have seamlines printed on them.

NOTCHES. Diamond shapes along the cutting line, used for matching seams. They may be numbered in the order in which the seams are joined.

BUTTON AND BUTTONHOLE PLACEMENT MARKS. Solid lines indicate the length of the buttonhole, if you are using the button size suggested on the pattern back. "X" or a button symbol shows the button size and placement.

DETAIL POSITIONS. Broken or solid lines indicating the placement for pockets or other details. Mark the position for accurate placement.

HEMLINE. Hem allowance is printed on the cutting line. Turn the hem up the specified amount, adjusting as necessary.

Pattern Layout continued

Prepare a large work area, such as a dining room table covered with a cutting board (page 19). Assemble all the pattern pieces you will be needing, and press out any wrinkles with a warm, dry iron.

Locate and circle the correct cutting layout diagram (page 31) on your pattern guide sheet. These diagrams usually show you the easiest, most efficient way to lay out your pattern. Some fabrics have a nap, meaning they have definite up and down directions. For these fabrics, pattern pieces must all be laid out in the same direction. **Fold the fabric in half, lengthwise.** Smooth it out on the work surface, so that the selvages align and the crosswise grain is perpendicular to them. Arrange the pattern pieces as indicated in the layout diagram. White pattern shapes indicate the piece is to be placed with the printed side up. Shaded pieces are to be placed with the printed side down. Be sure to follow any other incidental

directions that pertain to your layout. After all the pieces are in place, pin them to the fabric. Do not begin cutting until all the pattern pieces are in place.

PINNING

1 First, position the pattern pieces that are to be cut on the fold. Place each one directly on the folded edge of the fabric. Pin the corners

diagonally. Then continue pinning near the outer edge, placing the pins parallel to the cutting line. Space the pins about 3" (7.5 cm) apart; closer together on curves.

2 Place the straight-grain pattern pieces on the fabric, with the grainline arrow parallel to the selvages on woven fabrics or parallel to the ribs on knits. Measure from each end of the arrow to the selvage, shifting the pattern until the distances are equal. Pin both ends of the grainline so the pattern will not shift. Then pin the outer edges.

tell me more

FOLD THE FABRIC IN HALF, LENGTHWISE.

When your fabric is folded like this, you will end up with mirror-image pieces for the left and right sides of the garment. Pattern directions usually suggest folding right sides together. Sometimes there are advantages to folding wrong sides together, such as having a better view of the fabric design or ease in marking. Either way will work.

cutting and marking

Don't be intimidated! Locate the correct cutting lines, and cut with confidence. Transfer the necessary marks, and you'll be ready to sew!

CUTTING

Accuracy is important, since mistakes made in cutting cannot always be corrected. Before cutting, double-check the placement of the pattern pieces.

A Using bent-handled shears, cut with long, firm strokes, cutting directly on the cutting line. Take shorter strokes around curves. If you are using a multisize pattern, be sure that you follow the correct cutting line all the time.

B Notches can be cut outward, especially if the fabric is loosely woven or if the pattern calls for ¼" (6 mm) seam allowances. Cut multiple notches as one unit, not separately. Or, you can cut directly through the notches, and then mark them with short snips into the seam allowances.

C If you prefer to use a rotary cutter and mat, be sure to keep the mat under the area being cut. Use steady, even pressure, and, above all, keep fingers and small children away from the rotary cutter.

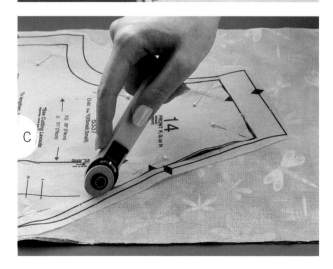

MARKING

Keep the pattern pieces pinned in place after cutting. Transfer pattern symbols to the appropriate side of the fabric, using one of the following methods.

A Pins are a quick way to transfer marks. Since they may fall out easily, use pin marks only when you intend to sew immediately. Or, pin-mark first, remove the pattern, and mark again, using chalk or erasable fabric marker.

B Erasable fabric markers are felt-tip pens designed specifically for sewing needs. Air-erasable marks disappear within 48 hours. Water-erasable marks disappear with a spritz of water.

C Chalk is available in pencil form or as a powder in a rolling wheel dispenser.

D Snips are handy for marking things like dots at shoulder seams. Make shallow snips into the seam allowances at the dot locations.

getting ready to sew

Simple tasks of inserting the needle, winding the bobbin, and threading the machine have tremendous influence on the stitch quality and performance of your machine. Use this guide as a general reference, but refer to your owner's manual for instructions specific to your machine.

INSERTING THE NEEDLE

Loosen the needle clamp. After selecting the appropriate needle for your project (page 12), insert it into the machine as high as it will go. The grooved side of the needle faces forward, if your bobbin gets inserted from the front or top; it faces to the left, if your bobbin gets inserted on the left. Tighten the clamp securely.

WINDING THE BOBBIN

If the bobbin case is built in, the bobbin is wound in place with the machine fully threaded as if to sew (page 40).

Removable bobbins are wound on the top or side of the machine, with the machine threaded for bobbin winding, as described in your owner's manual.

Bobbin thread must be drawn through the bobbin case tension spring. For wind-in-place bobbins, this happens automatically when you wind the bobbin, but you must do it manually when you insert a bobbin that already has thread on it.

After inserting the bobbin and threading the machine (page 40), you need to draw the bobbin thread to the top. Hold the needle thread while turning the handwheel toward you one full turn. As the needle goes down, the top thread interlocks with the bobbin thread and brings it up through the needle hole. Pull both threads together under the presser foot and off to the side or back.

THREADING THE MACHINE

Because every sewing machine is different, the threading procedure for your machine may differ slightly from the one shown here. Once again, it is important to refer to your owner's manual.

Every upper thread guide adds a little tension to the thread as it winds its way to the needle. Missing one of them can make a big difference in the quality of your stitches.

1 Spool spindle

2 Thread guide

5 Take-up lever

3 Tension guide

4 Thread guide

6 Thread guide

7 Needle

1 Set the thread spool on the spindle. For a vertical spindle, position the spool so that it will turn clockwise as you sew. If the spindle is horizontal, the spool is held in place with an end cap. If your spool has a small cut in one end for minding the thread, position the spool with that end to the right.

✂ **TIP** *If the spool is new and has paper labels covering the holes, poke them in, completely uncovering the holes, to allow the spool to turn freely. Unless your machine has a self-winding bobbin, you will want to wind the bobbin (page 38) before threading the machine.*

✂ **TIP** *It is very important to have the presser foot lever up when threading the machine because the tension discs are then open. If the presser foot is down and the discs are closed, the thread will not slide between the discs, and your stitches will not form properly.*

2 Pull thread to the left and through the first thread guide.

3 Draw thread through the tension guide.

4 Draw thread through the next thread guide.

5 Insert thread through the hole or slot in take-up lever.

6 Draw the thread through the remaining thread guides.

7 Thread the needle. Most needles are threaded from front to back; some, from side to side.

8 Holding the needle thread, turn the handwheel toward you one full rotation. The needle thread will engage the bobbin thread. When you tug on the needle thread, the bobbin thread should come up through the hole in the needle plate.

sewing a seam

Little frustrations, such as thread jams, erratic stitching lines, or having the thread pull out of the needle at the start of a seam, can often be prevented or corrected by following these basic guidelines.

HOW TO SEW A SEAM

1 Thread your machine (page 40) and insert the bobbin (page 12). Holding the needle thread with your left hand, turn the handwheel toward you until the needle has gone down and come back up to its highest point. You will feel a tug on the needle thread. Pull on the needle thread to bring the bobbin thread up through the hole in the throat plate. Pull both threads together under the presser foot and off to one side.

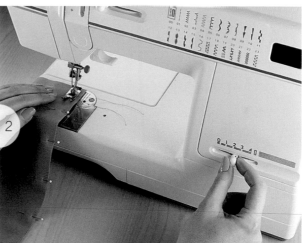

2 Cut rectangles of fabric. Place the pieces right sides together, aligning the outer edges. Pin the pieces together along one long edge, **inserting the pins** about every 2" (5 cm), **perpendicular to the edge**. Place the fabric under the presser foot so the pinned side edges align to the ½" (1.3 cm) seam allowance guide and the upper edges align to the back of the presser foot. Lower the presser foot, and set your stitch length at 2.5 mm, which equals 10 stitches per inch.

3 Backstitch several stitches to the upper edge of the fabric. Hold the thread tails under a finger for the first few stitches. This prevents the needle thread from being pulled out of the needle and also prevents the thread tails from being drawn down into the bobbin case, where they could potentially cause a thread jam.

4 Stitch forward over the backstitched line, and continue sewing the ½" (1.3 cm) seam. Gently guide the fabric while you sew by walking your fingers ahead of and slightly to the sides of the presser foot. Remember, you are only guiding; let the machine pull the fabric.

5 Stop stitching and **remove pins as you come to them**. When you reach the end of the fabric, stop stitching; backstitch several stitches, and stop again. Turn the handwheel toward you until the needle is in its highest position.

6 Raise the presser foot. Pull the fabric smoothly away from the presser foot, either to the left side or straight back. If you have to tug the threads, turn your handwheel slightly toward you until they pull easily. Cut the threads, leaving tails 2½" to 3" (6.5 to 7.5 cm) long.

tell me more

INSERTING THE PINS PERPENDICULAR TO THE EDGE. This makes it much easier to remove them as you sew. The pin heads are near the raw edge where you can easily grasp them with your right hand. In this position, you are much less likely to stick yourself with a pin as you sew.

REMOVE PINS AS YOU COME TO THEM. As tempting as it may be, don't sew over pins! You may be lucky and save a few seconds, or you could hit a pin and break your needle, costing you much more time in the long run.

how to balance tension

Your machine forms stitches by interlocking the bobbin thread with the needle thread. Every time the needle goes down into the fabric, a sharp hook catches the needle thread and wraps the bobbin thread around it. Imagine this little tug-of-war. If the needle thread tension is "stronger" than the bobbin thread tension, the needle thread pulls the bobbin thread through to the top. If the bobbin thread tension is "stronger," it pulls the needle thread through to the bottom. When the tensions are evenly balanced, the stitch will lock exactly halfway between the top and bottom of the layers being sewn, which is right where you want it.

Some machines have "self-adjusting tension," meaning the machine automatically adjusts its tension with every fabric you sew. For machines that do not have this feature, you may have to adjust the needle thread tension slightly as you sew different fabrics.

1 Thread your machine and insert the bobbin, using two very different colors of thread, neither of which matches the fabric. Cut an 8" (20.5 cm) square of a smooth, mediumweight fabric. Fold the fabric in half diagonally, and place it under the presser foot so the fold aligns to your ½" (1.3 cm) seam guide. Lower the presser foot and set your stitch length at ten stitches per inch or 2.5 mm long.

2 Stitch a line across the fabric, stitching ½" (1.3 cm) from the diagonal fold. Remove the fabric from the machine. Inspect your stitching line from both sides. If your tension is evenly balanced, you will see only one color on each side. If you see both thread colors on the top side of your sample, the needle tension is tighter than the bobbin tension. If you see both thread colors on the back side of your sample, the bobbin tension is tighter than the needle tension.

3 Pull on your stitching line until you hear threads break. (Because you stitched on the bias, the fabric will stretch slightly.) If the thread breaks on only one side, your machine's tension is tighter on that side.

Top tension too tight

Top tension too loose

Tension even

ADJUSTING THE TENSION

Before adjusting the tension on your machine, first check:

- that your machine is properly threaded (page 40)

- that your bobbin is properly installed

- that your needle is not damaged and is inserted correctly

After checking these three things, you may need to adjust the tension on your machine. (Check your owner's manual.) Tighten or loosen the needle thread tension slightly to bring the needle thread and bobbin thread tensions into balance. Test the stitches after each adjustment, until you achieve balanced tension. If slight adjustments of the needle tension dial do not solve the problem, the bobbin tension may need adjusting. However, most manufacturers do not recommend that you adjust bobbin tension yourself, so unless you have received instructions for adjusting the bobbin tension on your machine, take your machine in for repair.

SEAM FINISHES

A **Stitched and pinked finish.** Stitch ¼" (6 mm) from each seam allowance edge, using a straight stitch set at 12 stitches per inch, which equals 2 mm. Trim close to the stitching, using pinking shears (page 17). This finish is suitable for finely woven fabrics that do not ravel easily.

B **Zigzag finish.** Set the zigzag stitch on or near maximum width and a length of 10 stitches per inch, which equals 2.5 mm. Stitch close to the edge of each seam allowance so that the right-hand stitches go just over the edge. If the fabric puckers, try a narrower zigzag width.

C **Multistitch-zigzag finish.** If your machine has this stitch, check your owner's manual for directions on selecting the settings. Stitch near, but not over the edge of, each seam allowance.

D **Turn and zigzag finish.** Set the zigzag stitch near maximum width at a length of 10 stitches per inch, which equals 2.5 mm. Turn under the seam allowance edge ⅛" to ¼" (3 to 6 mm). Stitch close to the folded edge so that the right-hand stitches go just on or over the fold. Use this finish on loosely woven fabrics, especially on garments, such as jackets, where the inside may be visible occasionally.

TIP *Straight stitching lines are easier to achieve if you watch the edge of the fabric along the seam guide and ignore the needle. Sew smoothly at a relaxing pace, with minimal starting and stopping, and without bursts of speed. You have better control of the speed if you operate your foot control with your heel resting on the floor.*

SPECIAL SEAMS

Aside from the standard straight-stitch seam, your machine is probably capable of sewing several other stitches that are appropriate for various fabrics and situations. Whenever you sew with knits, for example, you want a seam that will stretch with the fabric. To prevent raveling of woven fabrics, seam allowance edges must be finished. There are several finishing methods to choose from, depending on the fabric and the capabilities of your machine. These general guidelines will help you decide when to use these stitches and finishing methods. Your owner's manual is the best source of specific information for your machine.

STRETCH SEAMS

Double-stitched seam (A). Stitch on the seam-line, using a straight stitch set at a length of 12 stitches per inch, which equals 2 mm long. Stretch the fabric slightly as you sew, to allow the finished seam to stretch that much. Stitch again ⅛" (3 mm) into the seam allowance. Trim the seam allowance close to the second stitching line. This seam is appropriate for fabrics with minimal stretch or for seams sewn in the vertical direction on moderate stretch knits.

Narrow zigzag seam (B). Stitch on the seam-line, using a very narrow zigzag stitch set at 12 stitches per inch, which equals 2 mm long. If the fabric is very stretchy in the direction you are sewing, you may also stretch the fabric slightly as you sew. Trim the seam allowance to ¼" (6 mm), if necessary. Set the zigzag wider, and stitch the seam allowance edges together. This seam is appropriate for very stretchy knits.

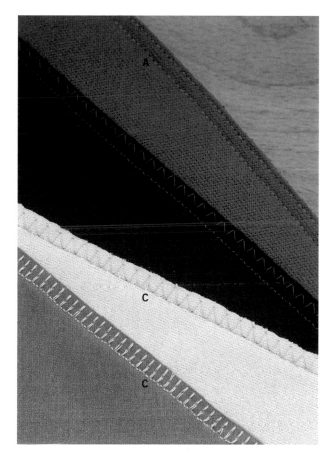

Built-in stretch stitch (C). Differing from brand to brand, these stitches are designed to incorporate stretch, so that you do not need to stretch the fabric as you sew. Some stitch styles, like the bottom two samples, are a pattern of zigzag and straight stitches that stitch and finish the seam in one pass. Check your manual for stitch settings.

TIP *The cut edges of knit fabrics do not ravel, but they often curl. To minimize this problem, the seam allowances are usually finished together and pressed to one side.*

hand stitches

While modern sewers rely on sewing machines for speedy construction, there are situations when hand stitching is necessary or preferable. You may need to slipstitch an opening closed to finish a pillow, or perhaps you like the look of a hand-stitched blind hem on a skirt. Of course you'll also need to sew on buttons.

THREADING THE NEEDLE

Insert the thread end through the needle's eye, for sewing with a single strand. Or fold the thread in half, and insert the fold through the eye, for sewing with a double strand. Pull through about 8" (20.5 cm). Wrap the other end(s) around your index finger. Then, using your thumb, roll the thread off your finger, twisting it into a knot.

✂ **TIP** *Use a single strand when slipstitching or hemming. Use a double strand when sewing on buttons. To avoid tangles, begin with thread no longer than 18" (46 cm) from the needle to the knot. Run the thread through beeswax (page 15), if desired.*

SLIPSTITCHING

1 Insert the threaded needle between the seam allowance and the garment, just behind the opening. Bring it to the outside in the seamline. If you are righthanded, work from right to left; lefties work from left to right.

2 Insert the needle into the fold just behind where the thread came up, and run it inside the fold for about ¼" (6 mm). Bring the needle out, and draw the thread snug. Take your next stitch in the opposite fold, inserting the needle directly across from the previous stitch.

3 Continue, crossing from one fold to the other, until you have sewn past the opening. Secure the thread with several tiny stitches in the seamline. Then take a long stitch, and pull it tight. Clip the thread at the surface, and let the tail disappear inside.

SEWING ON A SEW-THROUGH BUTTON

1 Place the button on the mark, with the holes lining up parallel to the buttonhole. Bring the needle through the fabric from the underside and up through one hole in the button. Insert the needle into another hole and through the fabric layers.

2 Slip a toothpick, match, or sewing machine needle between the thread and the button to form a shank. Take three or four stitches through each pair of holes. Bring the needle and thread to the right side under the button. Remove thetoothpick.

3 Wind the thread two or three times around the button stitches to form the shank. Secure the thread on the right side under the button, by making a knot or taking several small stitches. Clip the threads close to the knot.

SEWING ON A SHANK BUTTON

1 Place the button on the mark, with the shank hole parallel to the buttonhole. Secure the thread on the right side of the garment with a small stitch under the button.

2 Bring the needle through the shank hole. Insert the needle down through the fabric and pull the thread through. Take four to six stitches in this manner.

3 Secure the thread in the fabric under the button by making a knot or by taking several small stitches. Clip the thread ends.

hems

There are a number of ways to hem the lower edges of skirts, pants, jackets, and shirts. Some hems are sewn by machine; others by hand. The method you choose will depend on the fabric, the garment style, and your own preference. For methods that do not involve turning under the raw edge, finish the edge (page 46) in an appropriate manner, before hemming.

HAND HEMS

A **Blindstitch.** Fold back the finished edge of the hem ¼" (6 mm). Take a small stitch to anchor the thread in a seam allowance. Work with the needle pointing in the direction you are going. Take a very small horizontal stitch in the garment, catching only one or two threads. Take the next stitch in the hem, ¼" to ½" (6 mm to 1.3 cm) away from the first stitch. Continue alternating stitches; do not pull too tightly.

B **Blind catchstitch.** Fold back the finished edge of the hem ¼" (6 mm). Take a small stitch to anchor the thread in a seam allowance. Work with the needle pointing in the direction opposite from the way you are going. Take a very small horizontal stitch in the garment, catching only one or two threads. Take the next stitch in the hem, ¼" to ½" (6 mm to 1.3 cm) away from the first stitch, crossing the stitches. Continue alternating the stitches in a zigzag pattern.

C **Slipstitch.** Fold under the raw edge ¼" (6 mm), and press. Take a small stitch to anchor the thread in a seam allowance. Work with the needle pointing in the direction you are going. Follow the directions for slipstitching on page 49, catching only one or two threads with each stitch that goes into the garment.

MACHINE HEMS

A **Machine blindstitch.** Follow your manual for adjusting the stitch settings, and use the appropriate presser foot. Test the stitch on a scrap of the garment fabric until you are happy with the results. (A) Place the hem allowance facedown on the machine bed, with the bulk of the garment folded back. Allow about ¼" (6 mm) of the hem edge to extend under the presser foot, aligning the soft fold to rest against the guide in the foot. Stitch along the hem, close to the fold, catching only one or two threads of the garment with each left-hand stitch of the needle.

B When complete, open out the hem, and press it flat.

C **Double-fold hem.** This method results in one or two rows of straight stitches showing on the right side. Turn under a double-fold hem. Then stitch along the inner fold and repeat at the outer fold, if desired. This method is most successful on straight edges where there is no excess fullness to ease in.

D **Double-needle hem.** Stitched from the right side of the fabric, this hem is suitable for knit garments, because it will stretch slightly. The farther apart the needles are spaced, the more stretch the hem will have. However, widely spaced needles will usually produce a ridge between the stitching lines. Using two thread spools on top, thread both needles. Place tape on the bed of the machine as a stitching guide.

cutting decorator fabrics

Cutting into a new piece of fabric may seem a little scary, considering the investment you have just made. Here are a few guidelines for accurate cutting that should boost your confidence.

After preshrinking, straighten the cut ends of the fabric, using one of the three methods opposite. Then mark the other cutting lines, using the straightened edge as a guide. Before cutting full-width pieces of fabric for large home décor projects, such as tablecloths, duvet covers, or Roman shades, pin-mark the placement of each cut along the selvage. Mark out pieces for smaller projects, like decorator pillows or napkins, with chalk. Double-check your measurements and inspect the fabric for flaws. Once you have cut into the fabric, you cannot return it. To ensure that large décor items will hang or lay straight, the fabric lengths must be cut on-grain. This means that the cuts are made along the exact crosswise grain of the fabric. Patterned decorator fabrics are cut following the pattern repeat rather than the grainline so they must be **printed on-grain**.

A For tightly woven fabrics without a matchable pattern, mark straight cuts on the crosswise grain, using a carpenter's square. Align one edge to a selvage and mark along the perpendicular side.

B For loosely woven fabrics, such as linen tablecloth fabric, pull out a yarn along the crosswise grain, from selvage to selvage. Cut along the line left by the missing yarn.

C For tightly woven patterned decorator fabric, mark both selvages at the exact same point in the pattern repeat. Using a long straightedge, draw a line connecting the two points. If you will be stitching two or more full widths of fabric together, make all the cuts at the same location in the repeat. This usually means that you cut the pieces longer than necessary, stitch them together, and then trim them to the necessary length.

tell me more

PRINTED ON-GRAIN. This means the pattern repeat coincides exactly with the crosswise grain of the fabric. To test fabric before you buy, place it on a flat surface and fold the cut edge back, aligning the selvages on the sides. Crease the fold with your fingers, then unfold the fabric and check to see if the crease runs into the selvage at exactly the same point in the pattern on both sides. Slight differences of less than 2" (5 cm) can usually be corrected by stretching the fabric diagonally. Avoid buying fabric that is printed more that 2" (5 cm) off-grain, as you will not be able to correct it, and the finished project will not hang straight.

matching designs

Stitching seams in decorator fabrics that have printed designs or woven-in patterns requires a few extra steps to make sure the pattern will flow uninterrupted from one fabric width to the next.

1 Place two fabric widths right sides together, aligning the selvages. Fold back the upper selvage until the pattern matches. Adjust the top layer slightly up or down so that the pattern lines up exactly. Press the foldline.

2 Unfold the pressed selvage, and pin the fabric widths together, inserting the pins in and parallel to the foldline.

3 Turn the fabric over, and check the match from the right side. Make any necessary adjustments.

4 Repin the fabric so the pins are perpendicular to the foldline. Stitch the seam following the foldline; **remove pins as you come to them** (p. 43).

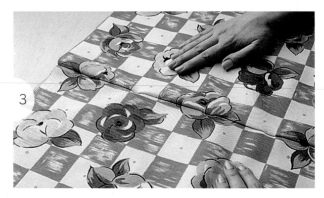

5 Check the match from the right side again. Make any necessary adjustments. Trim away the selvages, cutting the seam allowances to ½" (1.3 cm).

6 Set the pattern selector to **zigzag** and your stitch width and length to medium. **Finish the raw edges together** by zigzagging down the length of the seam. Press the seam allowances to one side.

7 Trim the entire fabric panel to the necessary cut length as determined in the project instructions. (Remember your initial cut length for the patterned fabric included extra length to accommodate the pattern repeat.)

tell me more

ZIGZAG. The sewing machine needle moves from side to side with each stitch. You can adjust the width and length of the zigzag. Experiment with different settings on a scrap of fabric.

FINISH THE RAW EDGES TOGETHER. This prevents the fabric from raveling, which is especially important for home décor items that are not lined.

PROJECTS

The eight projects in this section include easy home décor items and basic wardrobe pieces. In each project, you will learn a few new sewing skills. If you work your way through the projects in order, your skill set will be fairly complete by the time you finish your first unlined jacket. As you repeat techniques you've learned in previous projects, your confidence will grow.

Four of the garment projects require a commercial pattern, so look for a pattern that closely resembles the lines and detail level of the garment shown. Certainly you should read the pattern instructions, but use the book instructions and photographs to help you sew your garment. You do not need a commercial pattern to sew the tablecloth, pillow, baby blanket, or apron.

RECTANGULAR TABLECLOTH

A simple rectangular tablecloth adds elegance or accents your color scheme and is easily changed for special occasions, the changing seasons, or your mood! The neatly mitered corners look very professional, yet they are surprisingly easy to sew. This technique can be used for several other home decorating items, such as a square table topper to place over a floor-length round tablecloth, dinner napkins, placemats, or a table runner.

HOW TO SEW A RECTANGULAR TABLECLOTH

1 Determine the desired finished size for your tablecloth; add 4" (10 cm) to both length and width for the hem. Cut a rectangle of fabric equal to these measurements, following the cutting guidelines on pages 54 and 55.

TIP *Select fabric that is wide enough for your tablecloth to be sewn in one piece. 48" (122 cm) fabric for a finished width up to 44" (112 cm), 54" (137 cm) fabric for a finished width up to 50" (127 cm), or 60" (152.5 cm) fabric for a finished width up to 56" (142 cm).*

MATERIALS

○ Fabric, amount determined in step 1

○ Thread

○ Fabric glue stick

MATERIALS

○ Fabric, amount determined in step 1

○ Thread

○ Fabric glue stick

SKILLS

○ Sew double-fold hems

○ Use a glue stick to help make perfect mitered corners

2" (5 cm) for hem

Finished width

Finished length

(continued)

2 Press under 2" (5 cm) on all four edges of the cloth. Unfold the pressed edges and press each corner diagonally at the point where the creases intersect. Trim off the corner diagonally at the points where it crosses the foldlines. Use a dot of fabric glue stick to hold the corner in place.

3 Turn each cut edge in, aligning it to the first fold line, and press the outer fold.

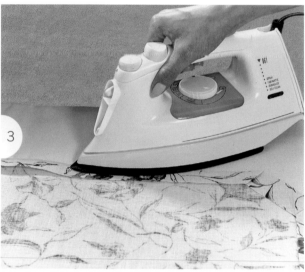

4 Refold on the first fold line, encasing the raw edge to form a 1" (2.5 cm) double-fold hem. Pin the hem in place, **inserting pins perpendicular to the folds** (p. 19). Use additional dots of glue stick to secure the mitered folds in the corners.

5 **Edgestitch** along the inner fold line. At the corners, stop with the needle down in the fabric and pivot. Overlap the stitches ½" (1.3 cm) where they meet. Press the tablecloth.

TIP *Support the bulk of the fabric to your left with a card table or other surface, so the fabric feeds easily as you stitch. This will help you maintain a nice straight stitching line.*

tell me more

EDGESTITCH. Stitch as close as possible to the inner edge of the hem. Align the presser foot so that the needle will enter the fabric just inside the inner edge. Note the point on the presser foot that aligns to the edge of the hem itself. As you sew, watch the fabric as it passes under that point on the foot rather than watching the needle. Stitch slowly for the best control.

KNIFE-EDGE PILLOWS

The knife-edge pillow is probably the most versatile style for decorating your home. There are no limits to the variations you can create, not only in size, color, and texture, but also in added details that give your pillow a personal touch. The directions that follow are for a knife-edge pillow that is 14" (35.5 cm) square. For your first knife-edge pillow, we recommend a firmly woven mediumweight fabric.

Ready-made knife-edge pillow inserts come in a wide selection of sizes, including 12", 14", 16", 18", 20", 24", and 30" (30.5, 35.5, 40.5, 46, 51, 61, and 76 cm) squares and a 12" × 16" (30.5 × 40.5 cm) rectangle. By adapting these cutting instructions, you can sew a cover for any size pillow insert. You can also use these instructions to sew your own pillow inserts in any size you like, stuffing them to a plumpness that pleases you.

HOW TO SEW A KNIFE-EDGE PILLOW

1 Cut two 15" (38 cm) squares of fabric, aligning the sides to the fabric grainlines (page 22). A ½" (1.3 cm) seam allowance is needed on each side, so 1" (2.5 cm) is added to each dimension of the **desired finished size.**

tell me more

DESIRED FINISHED SIZE. To make a knife-edge pillow of a different size, simply cut your fabric 1" (2.5 cm) larger in both directions than the desired finish d size of your pillow. Cut 17" (43 cm) squares for a 16" (40.5 cm) pillow; cut 13" × 19" (33 × 48.5 cm) rectangles for a 12" × 18" (30.5 × 46 cm) pillow.

(continued)

MATERIALS

○ 14" (35.5 cm) square pillow form
○ ½ yd. (0.5 m) of fabric
○ Matching thread
○ Hand-sewing needle

SKILLS

○ Backstitch
○ Set and press seams
○ Sew perfect corners
○ Slipstitch an opening closed by hand

2 Place the pillow front over the pillow back, right sides together, and align all four edges. Pin the layers together near the outer edges, **inserting the pins perpendicular to the edges** (p. 42). In the center of one side, leave a 7" (18 cm) opening unpinned.

3 Place the fabric under the presser foot, just ahead of the opening. Align the cut edges of the fabric to the ½" (1.3 cm) seam allowance guide on the bed of your machine. Remove the pin that marks the opening, before lowering the presser foot.

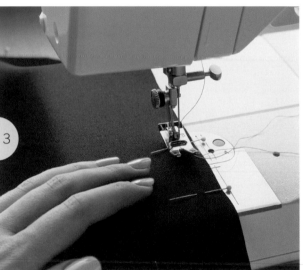

4 Backstitch three or four stitches; stop. Then, stitching forward, stitch the seam on all four sides, pivoting with the needle down at the corners. End the seam at the opposite side of the opening; backstitch three or four stitches.

5 Remove the fabric from the machine. Trim the threads close to the fabric. Press the seams flat to set the stitching line in the fabric. This may seem unnecessary, but it really does give you a better looking seam in the end.

✂ **TIP** *Most machines have a handy thread cutter located within a few inches (centimeters) of the presser foot. By using this thread cutter, you are also pulling enough thread through the needle and up from the bobbin to help you prevent a thread jam at the start of your next seam.*

(continued)

6 Turn back the top seam allowance, and press, applying light pressure with tip of the iron down the crease of the seam. In the area of the opening, turn back and press the top seam allowance ½" (1.3 cm).

7 Turn the cover over; turn back and press the remaining opening seam allowance.

8 To turn a **perfect corner**, fold in the seam allowances from one edge, and then fold in the seam allowances from the adjacent edge over them. Slip four fingers through the pillow opening and pinch the folded corner between your thumb and one finger. Turn that corner through the opening. Repeat with the other three corners. Your pillow cover has now been turned right side out.

9 Compress and insert the pillow form. Align the pressed edges of the opening, and pin the opening closed. Thread a hand needle and tie a knot in the end.

10 Slipstitch the opening closed, following the instructions on page 49.

tell me more

PERFECT CORNER. The corners of your pillow should be sharply squared, not rounded. To improve the appearance of a slightly rounded corner, you can push a pointed utensil into the corner from inside the pillow cover to force the stitches out to the corner. An inexpensive specialty tool, called a point turner (page 20), works well; or you can use a chop stick, a ballpoint pen with the ink ball retracted, or something similar. Use light pressure, though, so that you don't punch a hole in the corner.

ZIPPER CLOSURES

Pillows that get tossed around, leaned upon, and slid across the floor need occasional cleaning. A zipper closure sewn into a seam makes it much easier to remove and reinsert the pillow form. Any knife-edge pillow can be made with a zipper closure. Cut the fabric and prepare the pillow front and back according to the directions in the project. Then follow these directions to complete the pillow.

Purchase a conventional polyester coil zipper (not a separating style) to match your fabric, in the size indicated in the chart below.

HOW TO SEW A ZIPPER CLOSURE

1 Place the pillow front over the pillow back, right sides together. Pin the side that will have the zipper. Center the zipper alongside the pinned edges, and mark the seam allowances just above and below the zipper stops.

TIP *For best results, select a side that was cut on the lengthwise grain of the fabric. The lengthwise grain is more stable and will have less tendency to stretch as you sew.*

2 Stitch a ½" (1.3 cm) seam from the upper edge to the mark, backstitching at the beginning and the end. Repeat at the lower edge. Leave the center section open.

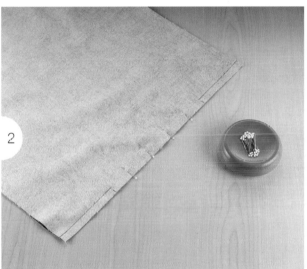

ZIPPER	PILLOW
7" (18 cm)	12" to 14" (30.5 to 35.5 cm)
9" (23 cm)	16" to 18" (40.5 to 46 cm)
12" (30.5 cm)	20" (51 cm) or larger

(continued)

3 **Machine-baste** on the seamline between the marks. Clip the basting stitches every 2" (5 cm) with a seam ripper. This will make the stitches easier to remove later

4 Press the seam flat; then press the seam allowances open. Finish the seam allowances with a zigzag stitch (page 46).

✂ **TIP** *If your fabric is loosely woven or tends to ravel easily, repeated washings could make the seam allowances ravel away and ruin your pillow. As a preventative measure, take the time to finish all of the seam allowances.*

5 Apply basting tape (page 21) to the right side of the zipper tape, running it along both outer edges.

6 Place the zipper facedown over the seam, with the zipper coil directly over the basted part of the seamline and the pull tab turned down. The zipper coil should be centered between the back-stitched areas. Press with your fingers to secure the zipper to the seam allowances.

🖎 *tell me more*
MACHINE-BASTE. Set the machine for the longest straight stitch possible. This stitching is temporary and will be easily removed later.

7 Spread the pillow pieces flat, right side up. Insert pins in the seamline, just above and below the zipper stops. Cut ½" (1.3 cm) transparent tape to fit between the pins; place it down the center of the seamline.

8 Attach the zipper foot and adjust it to the left of the needle. If your zipper foot is not adjustable, adjust the needle to the right of the foot. Stitch along the outer edge of the tape, stitching across one end, down one side, and across the other end; pivot at the corners.

9 Adjust the zipper foot to the right of the needle or adjust your needle to the left of the foot. Stitch over the previous stitches at one end, down the opposite side, and over the stitches at the other end. Clip the threads.

10 Remove the tape. Carefully remove the machine basting in the seamline, using a seam ripper.

11 Open the zipper. Pin the pillow front and back, right sides together, along the three remaining sides. Stitch ½" (1.3 cm) seam; press. Turn the pillow cover right side out and insert the pillow form through the zipper opening.

BABY BLANKET

Blankets serve many purposes in the routine of baby care. Most often they provide comfort, warmth, and security for little tykes. A blanket also provides a soft surface for rolling around on the floor or a make-do pad for a quick change when you're on the go. With easy-to apply blanket binding and synthetic fleece fabric, you can sew up new blankets in a jiffy. Because the following method involves the use of fabric glue, you'll want to launder the finished blanket before you use it.

HOW TO SEW A BABY BLANKET

1 Cut a rectangle of fabric 36" × 45" (91.5 × 115 cm). Use a quilting ruler or carpenter's square to ensure square corners. In the following steps, unroll the binding from the package as you need it, and don't cut it until step 7.

✂ **TIP** *Synthetic fleece is actually a knit fabric and is usually 60" (152.5 cm) wide. Avoid using either of the selvages as a side of your rectangle because they may be slightly stretched out of shape.*

(continued)

MATERIALS

○ 1 yd. (0.95 m) synthetic fleece

○ Satin blanket binding in color to match or coordinate with fabric

○ Quilting ruler or carpenter's square

○ Fabric glue stick (page 20)

○ Thread to match blanket binding

SKILLS

○ Apply satin blanket binding

○ Sew mitered corners

○ Careful pressing

2 Beginning about 10" (25.5 cm) from one corner and working toward the corner in a clockwise direction, slip the blanket edge between the layers of the binding. Tuck the edge in as close as possible to the binding fold. Insert pins through all the layers, perpendicular to the edge. Space the pins about 2" (5 cm) apart with the heads outward.

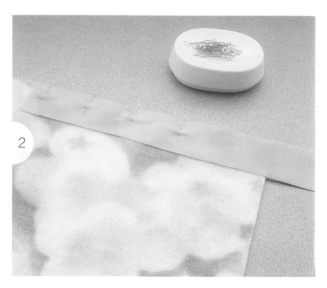

✂ **TIP** *Be sure to keep the binding folded smooth and flat over the edge, so that the outer crease remains sharp. This will ensure that the finished binding edges on the front and back of the blanket are perfectly aligned.*

3 Set the machine to sew a multistitch zigzag (page 46) at maximum width and 12 stitches per inch, which equals 2 mm. Place the blanket under the presser foot at the binding end, with the inner edge of the binding aligned to the **left side of the presser foot opening**. Stitch to the fabric edge, removing pins as you come to them. Stop, and remove the fabric from the machine.

tell me more

LEFT SIDE OF THE PRESSER FOOT OPENING. The opening in the center of the presser foot is more than wide enough to accommodate the widest stitch your machine can sew. Guide the fabric, keeping a tiny space between the binding edge and the left edge of the opening. The farthest left stitch of the needle should just stitch off the edge of the binding. Adjust the position slightly, if necessary.

4 Take the blanket to the ironing board. Open out the binding at the corner, and fold it down along the next side, so that the fabric edge aligns to the binding fold. A 45° angle will form in the binding. Press the angle lightly with the tip of the iron.

5 Fold the binding closed so that the angled fold forms a mitered corner. The fold runs diagonally from the outer corner to the inner corner, matching up perfectly.

(continued)

6 Flip the blanket over and miter the back of the binding so that the diagonal fold on the back also lines up perfectly. Using a fabric glue stick (page 20), secure the folds in place. This is called glue-basting.

7 Encase and pin the blanket edge to the next corner. Place the blanket under the presser foot, aligning the inner corner of the miter to the left side of the presser foot opening. Backstitch two or three stitches. Stitch forward to the fabric edge at the next corner. Stop, and remove the blanket from the machine.

8 Repeat steps 4 to 7 for the remaining corners. On the side where you started, cut the binding 4" (10 cm) beyond the beginning. Open the fold; press under 2" (5 cm) at the end.

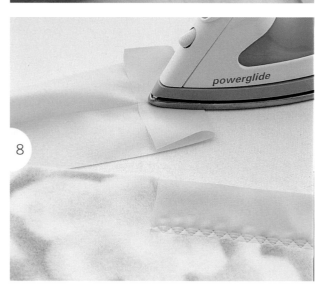

9 Refold and finish encasing and pinning the blanket edge. The folded end should overlap the cut end 2" (5 cm). Glue-baste the folded end in place. Stitch the last side, stitching about 1" (2.5 cm) beyond the overlap. Remove the blanket from the machine, and clip the threads.

10 **Reset the stitch length to 0**. Place the overlapped binding ends under the presser foot so that the fold is about ¼" (6 mm) ahead of the presser foot opening. Stitch in place until the needle has traveled from left to right at least twice. This tacking will keep the ends in place through many launderings.

tell me more

RESET THE STITCH LENGTH TO 0. The machine will still stitch side to side, as it is still set for multistitch-zigzag, but the fabric will not move forward.

ELASTIC-WAIST SKIRTS

Skirts with elastic waistbands are classic, comfortable, and easy-care. Straight or flared versions in varying lengths can be coordinated with a variety of sweaters or other tops for business, dress, or casual wear.

Check the pattern envelope for recommended fabrics. Some patterns are designed only for knits and generally fit the body closer, counting on the stretchiness of the fabric to allow you to slide the skirt over your hips. Patterns suitable for woven fabrics will include extra fullness. The first set of directions works for woven or knit fabrics. Alternate steps for sewing with knits begin on page 86. These directions may differ from your pattern; be sure to use the seam allowance given in your pattern. Select a pattern with two pieces: a front and a back. An elastic casing at the waistline is formed from excess fabric length at the skirt top. The skirt itself may be constructed of two, three, or four sections, depending on whether or not there are center front or back seams.

MATERIALS

- Skirt pattern with elastic waistline
- Fabric (check pattern for amount)
- Matching all-purpose thread
- 1" (2.5 cm) nonroll elastic, enough to go around your waist

SKILLS

- Sew elastic waistlines
- Hem a skirt
- Sew and finish seams

HOW TO SEW A PULL-ON SKIRT

1. To construct the skirt following these directions, 2¾" (7 cm) of fabric must be allowed for the casing above the waistline. This may be different from the casing allowance already on your pattern. Measure this distance from the waistline, and mark a cutting line on your pattern. (Add extra paper, if necessary.) Be sure to mark both front and back pattern pieces.

(continued)

2 Prepare the fabric (page 25), lay out the pattern (page 32), and cut the fabric (page 36). Transfer any necessary marks (page 37). Insert a size 11/70 or 12/80 sharp or universal sewing machine needle. If your pattern does not have center front or back seams, move on to step 4. If your pattern has a center front seam, place the skirt front pieces right sides together, aligning the center cut edges and matching the notches. Insert pins perpendicular to the center front seam.

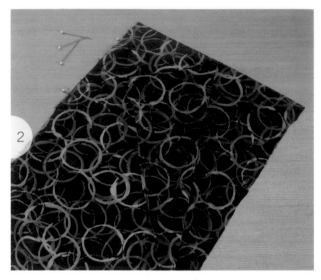

✂ **TIP** *Be sure you are not pinning the pieces together along the side seams. Sometimes it is difficult to tell the difference. Check your pattern to be sure.*

3 Place the fabric under the presser foot with the cut edges aligned to the ⅝" (1.5 cm) seam allowance guide. Stitch the center front seam, backstitching a few stitches at the upper and lower edges. If your pattern has a center back seam, stitch it in the same manner.

✂ **TIP** *If your skirt has side seam pockets, follow the pattern directions carefully because methods vary greatly.*

4 Place the front and back skirt pieces right sides together, aligning the side edges and matching the notches. **Insert pins perpendicular to the sides** (p. 43). Stitch the side seams, backstitching at the upper and lower edges, and **removing pins as you come to them** (p. 43). If you are sewing on a woven fabric, finish (page 46) the edges of all the seam allowances.

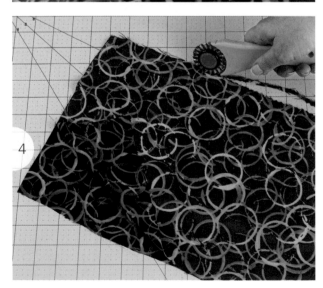

5 Press all the seams flat to set the stitching line in the fabric. This may seem unnecessary, but it really does give you a better-looking seam in the end. Then press the seam allowances open.

✂ **TIP** *To prevent the cut edge of the seam allowance from imprinting the front of the fabric, press seams open over a seam roll or hard cardboard tube.*

6 Baste the seam allowances open flat from the upper edge down about 4" (10 cm) (arrow). This will keep them from getting in the way when you insert the elastic in step 9. Finish the waistline edge, using a multistitch-zigzag (page 46). Fold the upper edge 1½" (3.8 cm) to the wrong side, and press. Insert pins along and perpendicular to the fold.

7 Edgestitch close to the fold around the upper edge of the waistline. Begin and end at a side seam, overlapping the stitches about ½" (1.3 cm).

(continued)

8 Insert pins along the lower edge of the casing. Place a piece of tape on the bed of your machine 1¼" (3.2 cm) from the tip of the needle. Stitch the lower edge of the casing, guiding the upper edge along the tape. Leave a 2" (5 cm) opening at one side seam.

✂ **TIP** *Sometimes it is difficult to tell the skirt front from the back when the garment is finished. We've sewn a short loop of twill tape under the casing seam to identify the back.*

9 Fasten a safety pin or bodkin (page 19) to one end of the elastic, and insert the elastic through the casing opening. Push and pull the safety pin all the way to the opposite side of the opening. Remove the basting threads from step 6.

✂ **TIP** *Insert a large safety pin across the free end of the elastic so that it will not get pulled into the opening.*

10 Try on the skirt. Pull up the elastic to fit your waist snugly, yet comfortably; pin the ends together. Take off the skirt, and trim the overlapped ends to ½" (1.3 cm), if necessary.

11 Pull the pinned ends of the elastic several inches (centimeters) out of the casing. Place them under the presser foot, and stitch through both layers, using a multistitch-zigzag. To reinforce, stitch again.

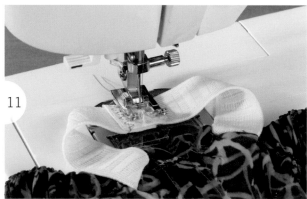

12 Machine-stitch the opening in the casing closed. Distribute the casing fullness evenly around the elastic. **Stitch in the ditch** at the seams (arrow) to keep the elastic from shifting or rolling.

13 Try on the skirt, and have someone **mark the hem length** for you, using chalk or pins. Take off the skirt, and trim the hem allowance to an even depth. (Check the pattern for hem allowance.) Turn under the hem along the markings, and pin. Press. For double-fold hems on slightly flared skirts, it is helpful to hand-baste on the inner fold.

14 Stitch the hem by hand (page 52) or by machine (page 53); select a method that will allow the hem to stretch, if you are using a knit. Give the skirt a final pressing, and give yourself a pat on the back.

tell me more

STITCH IN THE DITCH. Stitching from the right side and using short stitches, stitch directly into the well of the seam. Your stitches will practically disappear.

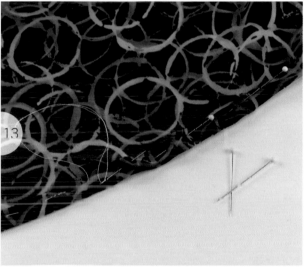

MARK THE HEM LENGTH. During the marking, stand straight, wearing the shoes you will be wearing with the skirt. The person marking should measure up from the floor to the desired length, moving around you as necessary. Otherwise, the hem will be uneven. If you don't have help, turn up the hem to the desired length all the way around and check in a mirror for even length.

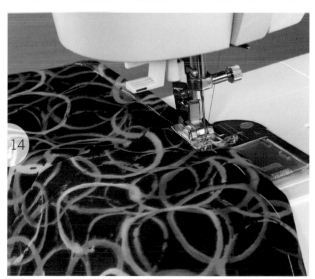

ALTERNATE STEPS FOR A KNIT PULL-ON SKIRT

1 To construct a knit skirt following these directions, an amount of fabric equal to **twice the width of the elastic** must be allowed above the waistline. Measure this distance from the waistline, and mark a new cutting line on your pattern. (Add extra paper, if necessary.) Be sure to mark both front and back pattern pieces. Follow steps 2 to 5 on pages 82 and 83, sewing with the seam allowances designated by your pattern. It is not necessary to finish seams on knit skirts.

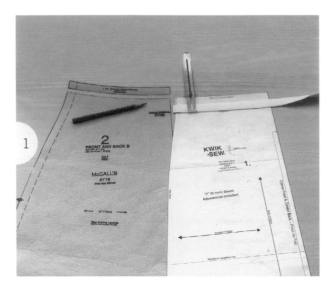

✂ **TIP** *Read your pattern directions. Some patterns, especially those that have ¼" (6 mm) seam allowances, instruct you to sew your elastic waistline with this method. There is no need to alter those patterns, as they already allow this amount of fabric at the top.*

2 Cut a piece of elastic that fits your waist snugly, yet still stretch to fit over your hips. Overlap the ends ½" (1.3 cm), and stitch them together, using a wide zigzag stitch or multistitch-zigzag. Divide both the elastic and the upper edge of the skirt into fourths, and pin-mark. Pin the elastic to the wrong side of the skirt, aligning the edges and matching the pin marks; insert the pins perpendicular to the edges.

3 Insert four more pins, evenly spaced, between the quarter marks, distributing the fabric fullness evenly. Set your machine for a medium-width multistitch-zigzag. Place the skirt under the presser foot with the elastic on top. Align the edge of the foot to the elastic and fabric edges. Stitch, **stretching the elastic to fit between the pins** and keeping the edges aligned. Remove pins as you come to them, stopping with the needle down in the fabric.

4 Fold the elastic to the wrong side of the skirt, so the fabric encases the elastic. From the right side of the skirt, **stitch in the ditch** (p. 85) of the seam through all the waistband layers, at each seam. This step makes step 5 easier.

✂ **TIP** *Stretch the waistband slightly to give yourself a clear view of your target.*

5 With the right side facing up, topstitch through all layers of the waistband, stretching the elastic as you sew. Use either a zigzag or multistitch-zigzag, with medium width and length, and stitch near the lower edge of the elastic. These stitches will allow the skirt to stretch as it goes over your hips. Finish the skirt, following steps 13 and 14 on page 85.

tell me more

TWICE THE WIDTH OF THE ELASTIC. For this method, 1" (2.5 cm) elastic works well, though you may decide to use a different width. Some specialty elastics have channels for topstitching, giving the look of multiple rows.

STRETCHING THE ELASTIC TO FIT BETWEEN THE PINS. Grasp the fabric and elastic behind the presser foot with one hand and ahead of the presser foot with the other hand, working in small sections at a time. Stretch the elastic only far enough to take up the slack in the fabric. Keep an even tension on the elastic, allowing the feed dogs to feed the fabric at a steady pace. Stop sewing to move your hands.

ELASTIC-WAIST PANTS

Pull-on pants with elastic waists are easy to fit and easy to sew. When sewn in supple, lightweight wovens, such as rayon or microfiber, they are elegant enough for evening wear. For sportier looks, cotton, cotton blends, linen, or seersucker work well and can be paired with simple T-shirts or blouses. Consider purchasing enough fabric to make a matching jacket to go with your pants and complete the outfit.

Select a pants pattern with two main pieces: the front and the back. The elastic casing for the waist is formed from excess fabric at the top. These instructions are for pants without pockets. The method for sewing side-seam pockets varies from pattern to pattern. Once you understand the basics of sewing pull-on pants, you can advance to a pattern with pockets, following the pattern instructions closely.

MATERIALS

- Pants pattern; loose-fitting with elastic waistline
- Fabric (check pattern for amount)
- Matching all-purpose thread
- ⅜" (1 cm) elastic, enough to go twice around your waist

SKILLS

- Alter the crotch length of a pattern
- Alter the leg length of a pattern
- Make a multi-row elastic waistband

The waistband casing on these pants is divided in half with a stitching line to accommodate two elastic strips.

HOW TO SEW PULL-ON PANTS

1 Measure the length of the crotch seam on a pair of pants that you know fits comfortably. Start from the bottom of the waistband in the front and measure the distance around the crotch to the bottom of the waistband in the back. On your pattern, measure the total crotch length, standing the tape measure on edge and measuring along the seamline of the center front and center back. Begin and end at the waistline mark; don't include the ⅝" (1.5 cm) seam allowances at the inseam.

2 Compare the pants crotch length to the pattern crotch length. Alter your pattern, if necessary. Cut the pattern pieces apart on the horizontal adjustment line. Then lap the pieces **by half the total amount needed** to shorten (left), or separate the pieces by half the total amount needed to lengthen (right). Insert a paper strip to lengthen; tape the pieces in place.

3 Next, compare the inseam measurements on your pants and on your pattern, measuring from the crotch seamline to the hemline. Make any necessary alteration at the horizontal adjustment line.

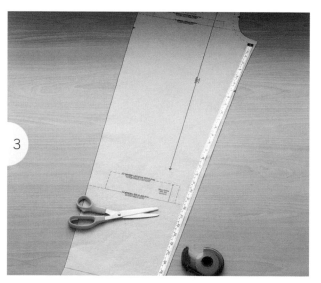

4 To construct the pants following these directions, 2¾" (7 cm) of fabric must be allowed for the casing above the waistline. Measure this distance from the waistline, and mark a new cutting line on your pattern. (Add extra paper, if necessary.) Be sure to mark both front and back pattern pieces.

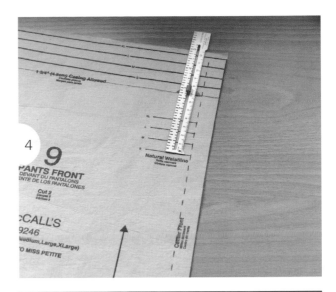

5 Prepare the fabric (page 25), lay out the pattern (page 32), and cut the fabric (page 36). Transfer any necessary marks (page 37). Set your sewing machine on a straight stitch of 10 to 12 stitches per inch, which is 2 to 2.5 mm. Insert a sewing machine needle suitable for your fabric (page 12). Place the right front over the right back, right sides together, along the inner leg. Pin them together, matching notches and **inserting the pins perpendicular to the edges** (p.43). Stitch the seam, using ⅝" (1.5 cm) seam allowance unless your pattern indicates another seam allowance. Repeat for the left front and back legs.

6 Finish the edges of the seam allowances (page 46). Press the seams flat; then press them open.

 tell me more
BY HALF THE TOTAL AMOUNT NEEDED.
For example, if you need to shorten the crotch 1" (2.5 cm), shorten the pants front ½" (1.3 cm), and shorten the pants back ½" (1.3 cm).

(continued)

7 With right sides together, pin the sewn right and left pants sections together at the crotch seam. Line up the inner leg seams, and match any notches. Stitch the entire seam. Then stitch the curved area of the seam between the notches a second time, ¼" (6 mm) from the first stitching.

8 Trim the seam in the curved area of the crotch close to the second stitching line. Finish the trimmed seam allowances. Then also finish the remaining seam allowances separately. Press the seam allowances open in the front and back, above the trimmed portion of the seam.

9 Pin the front and back, right sides together, at the side seams, matching notches and any other marks. Stitch a ⅝" (1.5 cm) seam from the bottom of the leg to the upper edge. Repeat for the other side seam.

10 Finish the seam allowances separately. Press the seams flat; then press them open, using a seam roll. Baste all the seam allowances open flat from the upper edge down about 4" (10 cm). This will keep them from getting in the way when you insert the elastic in step 15.

11 Finish the waistline (page 46). Fold the upper edge 1½" (3.8 cm) to the wrong side, and press. Insert pins along and perpendicular to the fold.

12 **Edgestitch** (p. 63) close to the fold around the upper edge of the waistline. Begin and end at a side seam, overlapping the stitches about ½" (1.3 cm).

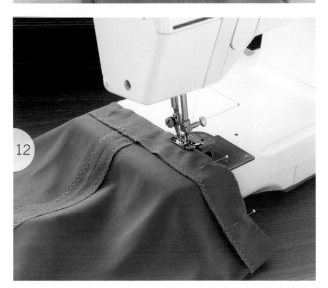

(continued)

13 Place a piece of tape on the bed of your machine 1¼" (3.2 cm) from the tip of the needle. Stitch the lower edge of the casing, guiding the upper edge along the tape. Leave a 2" (5 cm) opening at one side seam.

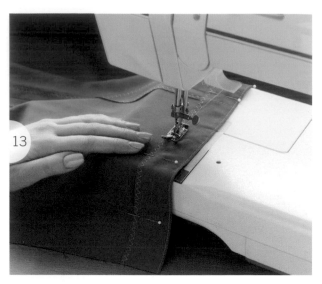

14 Measure from the upper edge of the waist to a point halfway between the two stitching lines. Place tape on the machine bed as a sewing guide. Stitch, leaving a 2" (5 cm) opening just above the first opening.

✂ **TIP** *To use three rows of ¼" (6 mm) elastic in your waistline casing, divide the space into even thirds.*

15 Cut two pieces of ⅜" (1 cm) elastic a little larger than your waist measurement. Fasten a safety pin or bodkin (page 19) to one end of one elastic, and insert the elastic through the casing opening into the top channel. Push and pull the safety pin through all the way to the opposite side of the opening, taking care not to let the free end disappear into the opening. Then do the same with the second piece of elastic, inserting it into the lower channel. Secure the ends of both pieces with safety pins.

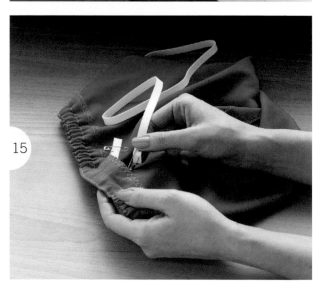

16 Try on the pants. Pull up the elastic to fit your waist snugly, yet comfortably; pin the ends together. Take off the pants. Pull the pinned ends of the top elastic several inches (centimeters) out of the casing. Trim the overlapped ends to ½" (1.3 cm), if necessary. Place them under the presser foot, and stitch through both layers, using a multistitch-zigzag. Repeat for the lower elastic.

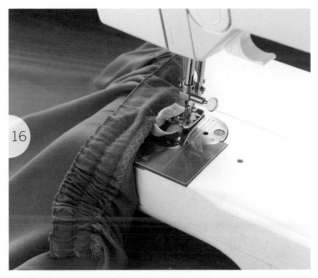

17 Machine-stitch the openings in the casing closed. Distribute the casing fullness evenly around the elastic. **Stitch in the ditch** (p. 85) at the seams to keep the elastic from shifting or rolling. Remove the basting stitches from step 10.

18 Turn under the hem allowance, and pin in place. Try on the pants, and adjust the length, if necessary. Take off the pants, and trim the hem allowance to an even depth. Press the fold. Finish the lower edge. Stitch the hem by hand (page 52) or by machine (page 53). Give the pants a final pressing, and they're ready to wear!

T-SHIRTS

T-shirts are classic and versatile; it seems you can never have too many. As you become more experienced, you'll be surprised how quickly you are able to make them. The fun begins in selecting your knit fabric (page 23) from the array of stripes, prints, and colorful solids available.

To help you decide which pattern to buy, note the way the T-shirts fit the models or sketches on the pattern envelope front. Some patterns are designed for an oversized look, others are meant to fit your body more closely. Your pattern should have four pieces: front, back, sleeve, and neck ribbing. Some may also have a piece for sleeve ribbing.

The fit of the T-shirt will vary with the fabric's degree of stretch. T-shirt patterns, designed for knits only, indicate the amount of stretch required of the fabric. For instance, "25% stretch crosswise" would indicate that 4" (10 cm) of fabric will stretch on the crosswise grain an additional 1" (2.5 cm). Always test the degree of stretch in the fabric, especially if you are making a close-fitting T-shirt.

MATERIALS

○ T-shirt pattern (designed for stretch knits)

○ Knit fabric (check pattern for amount)

○ Scraps of fusible knit interfacing (page 19)

○ Ribbing (check pattern for amount)

○ Matching all-purpose thread

SKILLS

○ Sew with knit fabric

○ Sew in sleeves

○ Apply ribbing to a neckline

HOW TO SEW A T-SHIRT

1 Prepare the fabric (page 25); however, don't wash the ribbing, as the raw edges are likely to stretch out of shape. T-shirts are easiest to sew using ¼" (6 mm) seam allowances. If your pattern pieces have ⅝" (1.5 cm) seam allowances, trim them down to ¼" (6 mm) before laying out the pattern. Lay out the pattern (page 32), and cut the fabric (page 36). Transfer any necessary marks (page 37). Insert a ballpoint sewing machine needle; size 11/70 or 12/80 is suitable for most knits. Cut two ½" (1.3 cm) strips of fusible interfacing the length of the shoulder seam. Place a strip even with the cut edge of each back shoulder, on the wrong side of the fabric. Fuse the strips in place, following the manufacturer's directions. This is done to **stabilize the shoulder seams**.

✂ **TIP** *The interfacing bolt is wrapped with a long sheet of plastic on which the directions are printed. Have the store clerk cut off a section of the directions for you to take home.*

2 Place the T-shirt front over the back, right sides together, aligning the shoulder seam allowance edges. Pin, inserting the pins perpendicular to the edges. Stitch the front and back T-shirt sections together at the shoulder seams, using a ¼" (6 mm) seam allowance; backstitch a few stitches at each edge. Since the shoulder seams are stabilized, a straight stitch is appropriate here.

3 Add a second row of machine stitching (either a straight stitch or a narrow zigzag) next to the first row, within the seam allowance. Press the shoulder seam allowances toward the shirt back.

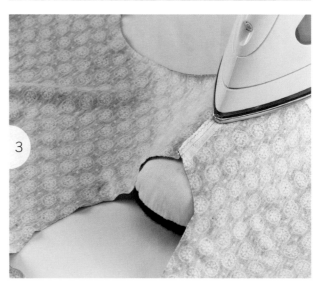

4 Mark the center front and center back of the neckline with pins. Then bring the two centers together and mark the points halfway between with pins. (These marks should be slightly ahead of the shoulder seams.) The neckline is now divided into fourths.

5 Sew the short ends of the **ribbing, right sides together**, forming a circle. Use ¼" (6 mm) seam allowance, and sew with a short straight stitch. Press the seam open with your fingers. Avoid pressing ribbing with an iron, as this may destroy its elasticity.

6 Fold the ribbing in half, lengthwise, with the raw edges even and the seam allowances on the inside. Divide the ribbing into fourths, as you did the neckline. Mark these sections with pins.

tell me more
STABILIZE THE SHOULDER SEAMS.
Shoulder seams follow the crosswise grain, the direction in which knit fabrics stretch the most. However, it is not desirable or necessary to have shoulder seams that stretch. Narrow strips of fusible interfacing help the seams keep their intended length. You'll also find that this makes sewing in the stretchy direction much easier.

RIBBING, RIGHT SIDES TOGETHER. Sometimes knit fabrics and ribbings do not have a right or wrong side. To test, gently stretch the raw edge on the crosswise grain of the ribbing. If the edge curls to one side, that side is the right side of the fabric. If it doesn't curl to either side, either side can be used on the outside.

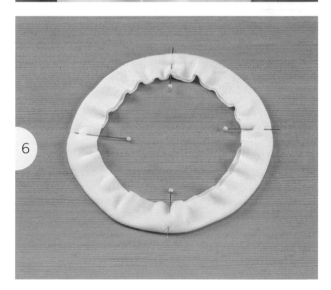

(continued)

7 Pin the ribbing to the right side of the neckline, aligning the ribbing seam to the center back pin mark; match up the remaining pin marks.

8 Place the fabric under the presser foot, with the ribbing facing up. Stitch with a narrow zigzag or stretch stitch (page 47), keeping the raw edges even and stretching the ribbing evenly to fit each section between pins. Remove the pins as you come to them.

9 Stitch again next to the first row, using a narrow, medium-length zigzag stitch. Gently press the ribbing toward the shirt, being careful not to stretch the ribbing.

10 Make sure you have marked the top ot the sleeve and any other notches on the sleeve and shirt as indicated on the pattern pieces. With right sides together, pin the sleeve to the armhole of the shirt, matching the top dot or notch to the shoulder seam, and aligning any other notches. Pin frequently, easing in any extra sleeve fullness.

11 Stitch the armhole seam, using a narrow, medium-length zigzag stitch; remove the pins as you come to them. Stitch again next to the first row, within the seam allowance.

12 Repeat steps 10 and 11 for the other sleeve. Press the seams toward the sleeves. With the right sides together, pin the shirt front to the shirt back along the sides and sleeves, matching the underarm seams.

13 Stitch and finish the seams in the same manner as for the sleeve seams, beginning at the lower edge of the shirt and sewing continuously to the lower edge of the sleeve. Press the seams toward the back.

✂ **TIP** *You can press the side seams, simply by slipping the shirt over the end of the ironing board. Insert a seam roll or sleeve board (page 18) into the sleeve, so you can press the seam allowance to the side without pressing unwanted creases into the opposite side of the sleeve.*

14 Turn under the lower **hem allowance**, as specified by your pattern. Stitch the hem by hand (page 52) or by machine (page 53); select a method that will allow the hem to stretch, if necessary. Hem the lower edges of the sleeves in the same manner.

tell me more

HEM ALLOWANCE. The pattern has allowed a predetermined extra length for turning under and finishing the sleeves and lower edge. This amount is indicated on your pattern.

APRON WITH POCKETS

With the renewed interest in cooking and retro fashions, aprons have made a grand comeback. Made from a washable fabric with a fun print, this apron has a skirt gathered to a waistband with ties attached. Contrasting fabric was used for the pockets, waistband, and ties. Rickrack trim applied to the pockets and skirt hem give the apron a retro look.

This style is made from six rectangles of fabric: a large rectangle for the skirt, two smaller rectangles for the pockets, two long narrow rectangles for ties, and one for the waistband. You don't need to buy a commercial pattern, you can simply measure and mark out the pieces on your fabric and cut them out.

HOW TO SEW AN APRON

1 Prepare the fabric (page 25). Lay out the fabric in a single layer. Using a carpenter's square or quilter's ruler, measure and mark out the rectangles listed below. Mark the skirt piece on one fabric; mark the waistband, pockets, and ties on the other fabric. Do not use a selvage as one of the sides. Cut out the pieces.

DIMENSIONS FOR APRON PIECES

Skirt	20" long x 30" wide (50.8 x 76.2 cm)
2 pockets	8½" long x 7½" wide (21.6 x 19.2 cm)
Waistband	4½" x 20" (11.4 x 50.8 cm)
2 ties	4½" x 28" (11.4 x 71.1 cm)
Waistband interfacing	2" x 19" (5.1 x 48.3 cm)

MATERIALS

- ⅝ yd. (0.6 m) lightweight woven fabric for skirt
- ½ yd. (0.5 m) lightweight contrasting fabric for pockets, waistband, and ties
- Lightweight fusible interfacing, 2" x 19" (5.1 x 48.3 cm)
- Matching all-purpose thread
- 1 package of wide rick rack
- Glue stick

SKILLS

- Gathering fabric
- Sewing a waistband
- Sewing double fold hems
- Sewing a patch pocket
- Applying decorative trims

(continued)

2 Fold upper edge of one pocket piece 1" (2.5 cm) to the wrong side and press. Unfold the edge and turn the raw edge in to meet the pressed fold; press again. Then refold the edge, and press again, forming a double-fold facing. Repeat for the other pocket.

3 Turn the facing to the right side of the pocket, even with the bottom fold. Pin the layers together at the sides. Starting at the top of the pocket, stitch a ½" (1.3 cm) seam to the bottom of the facing on each side of the pocket, backstitching at the beginning and end. **Trim the corners diagonally**. Trim the facing seam allowance to ¼" (6 mm)

4 Turn the facing to the inside. Using a point turner or similar tool, gently push out the corners to square them off. Press the top fold; the facing should be ½" (1.3 cm) wide. Fold in the sides ½" (1.3 cm), and press. To square the bottom corners, turn under ½" (1.3 cm) on the bottom, and press.

 tell me more
TRIM THE UPPER CORNERS DIAGONALLY.
This minimizes the excess bulk to form a smoother corner when the piece is turned back to the inside.

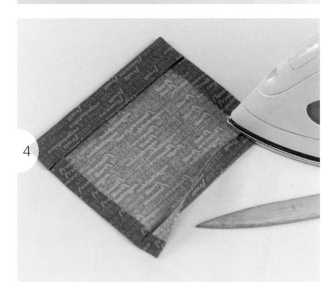

5 Find the ⅜" (1 cm) seam guide on the throat plate. For easier guiding, mark this distance from the needle on the machine bed, using tape. Topstitch the upper edge of the pocket, guiding the fold along the tape mark and catching the facing in the stitches.

6 Cut rick rack the width of the pocket plus 1¼" (3.2 cm). Apply glue stick to the back of the rick rack. Place the rick rack over the facing stitching line, wrapping the ends to the underside of the pocket. Stitch down the center of the rick rack, backstitching at the sides of the pocket. Repeat for other pocket.

7 Place the pockets on the apron skirt 9½" (24.1 cm) from the long bottom edge and 6" (15.2 cm) from the sides. Make sure the pocket edges are parallel to the skirt edges. Pin the sides and bottom edges of the pockets to the skirt, inserting the pins perpendicular to the pocket edges.

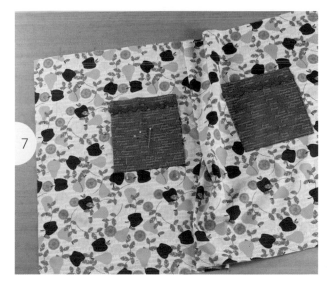

(continued)

8 With a pencil or erasable fabric marker, draw a small triangle in each upper corner of each pocket, ⅛" (3 mm) from the top and side edges. Place the skirt under the presser foot with the top of the pocket toward you, aligning the needle to start sewing at the lowest point of the triangle. Stitch forward two stitches, then backstitch two stitches. Now stitch diagonally to the top, pivot, and stitch a few stitches across the top of the triangle. Pivot again so the needle is now aligned to stitch down the side of the pocket. Edgestitch around the sides and the bottom of the pocket, and finish with the triangle on the opposite corner, again backstitching two stitches.

TIP *Apron pockets are used frequently. Stitching triangles at the top corners reinforces them better than merely backstitching, which can put more strain on the skirt fabric beneath the pocket.*

9 Turn under the lower edge of the skirt 2" (5.1 cm) and press. Unfold the edge and turn the raw edge in to meet the pressed fold; press again. Refold the edge, forming a 1" (2.5 cm) **double-fold hem**. Insert pins perpendicular to the folds.

10 At the bottom corner of the skirt, turn the hem to the right side, keeping the inner fold in place. Pin the layers together at the sides. Stitch a 1" (2.5 cm) seam across the hem, backstitching at the beginning and end. Trim the corner diagonally. Turn the corner right side out. Repeat for other side.

11 Fold and press ½" (1.3 cm) double-fold hems in the skirt sides, making the first fold 1" (2.5 cm) deep. Insert pins perpendicular to the folds.

12 Place the skirt, right side down, under the presser foot with the bulk of the fabric to the left of the machine. Beginning at the top of the side hem, stitch along the inner fold, removing pins as you come to them. Pivot at the top fold of the bottom hem, and stitch along the hem fold to the opposite side. Pivot again, and stitch along the inner fold of the other side hem to the skirt top.

13 Cut rick rack the width of the skirt plus 1¼" (3.2 cm). Apply rickrack over the stitching line of the bottom hem, following step 6.

14 Set your machine to sew long straight stitches. Beginning at one side hem, baste a scant ½" (1.3 cm) from the top edge of the skirt. Stitch from the right side of the fabric. Stop stitching at the opposite side hem. Stitch another row of long stitches ¼" (6 mm) closer to the edge. Leave thread tails at each end. Set the skirt aside.

tell me more

DOUBLE-FOLD HEM. Double-fold hems are made with two folds of equal depths, encasing the cut edge in the crease of the outer fold. Pressing the first fold to the total hem depth allows you to be more accurate in turning and pressing.

(continued)

15 Fold a tie lengthwise, with right sides together and raw edges even. Insert pins perpendicular to the edges. Stitch ½" (1.3 cm) seam across one end of the tie and the long edge. Trim corners diagonally. Repeat for the other tie. **Turn the ties right side out**. Press. Topstitch ⅛" (3 mm) from outside edges. Set the ties aside.

16 Press the waistband in half lengthwise, and unfold. Place the interfacing strip, fusible side down, on the wrong side of the waistband, aligning one long edge to the center crease and centering the strip lengthwise. Fuse the interfacing in place.

17 Press under ⅜" (1 cm) on the long unfused edge of the waistband. Mark the cut edge of the waistband ½" (1.3 cm) from each end. Then divide the waistband into four equal parts, and mark, using chalk pencil or erasable marker. Also divide the upper edge of the skirt into four equal parts, and mark.

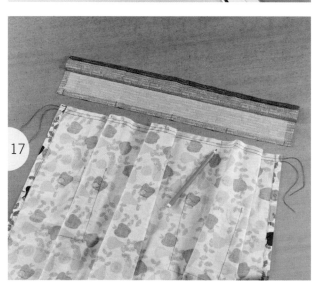

18 With right sides together, pin the cut edge of the waistband to the upper edge of the skirt, matching quarter marks. Insert pins from the skirt side. At one end, grasp both of the bobbin threads, and pull on them with equal tension, sliding the fabric along the thread to gather it.

19 Keep pulling on the bobbin threads, gathering the fabric, and distributing the gathers evenly between the pins on half of the waistband. When the skirt fabric is gathered up to fit that half, secure the bobbin threads by winding them in a figure eight around the end pin.

20 Pull the bobbin threads from the other end to gather the remaining half; secure the threads. Distribute all the gathered fabric evenly along the waistband, inserting pins frequently to hold the fabric in place.

tell me more

TURN THE TIES RIGHT SIDE OUT. There are special tools for turning narrow tubes inside out. Look for them at the fabric store. Because this is a frequently required task in sewing, it is worth it to buy one of these tools. In a pinch, you can probably get the job done by working the fabric over the eraser end of a pencil or a wooden spoon handle, but it's much harder to do.

18

19

20

(continued)

21 Reset the stitch length for 10 to 12 stitches per inch, which is 2 to 2.5 mm. Place the fabric under the presser foot, the waistband on the bottom. Stitch the waist seam ½" (1.3 cm) from the raw edges. Keep the gathers even and remove pins as you come to them.

22 Trim the seam allowances just above the gathering stitches.

23 Turn the seam allowance toward the waistband, and press lightly with the tip of the iron. Avoid pressing creases into the gathers.

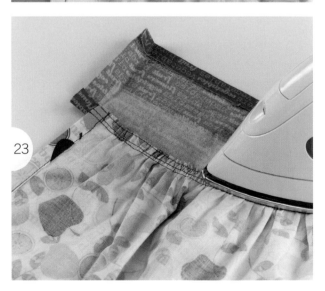

24 Pin the ties to the short ends of the waistband, right sides together. Fold the center crease of the waistband in the opposite direction over the ties, right sides together. Stitch a ½" (1.3 cm) seam across each end of the waistband. Trim the seams and clip the corners diagonally.

25 Turn the waistband right side out, encasing the raw ends of the ties. Press. The folded edge should extend down over the seam on the wrong side. From the right side, pin in the ditch of the waistband seam, catching the folded edge on the back.

TIP *Be sure to keep the seam allowance turned up as it was pressed. Check to be sure the folded edge of the waistband is pinned at a consistent depth and lies flat.*

26 **Stitch in the ditch** (p. 85) of the seam from the right side of the skirt, backstitching at the ends of the waistband and removing pins as you come to them. Be careful not to catch the ties in the stitching.

UNLINED JACKETS

Collarless jackets are versatile additions to any wardrobe. Those that are loose-fitting and unlined, with drop-shoulder styling and patch pockets, are easy to make. Look for a pattern that includes pieces for front, back, sleeve, front facing, back facing, and pocket.

These directions are for square bottom front corners. If your pattern has round corners, pay close attention to the pattern directions when attaching the facing (step 11) and hemming the lower edge (steps 24 to 27). As with any other project, the fabric of your jacket will determine whether it will be more suitable for casual, business, or dress. Cotton, cotton blends, and denim would be good choices to wear with jeans or casual slacks and skirts. Wool, wool blends, linen, and rayon work for business or dress. When you're feeling really confident, you might even consider making a jacket of suit-weight silk, like the one at left.

MATERIALS

- Jacket pattern; unlined, loose-fitting
- Fabric for jacket (check pattern for amount)
- Matching all-purpose thread
- Lightweight fusible interfacing (check pattern for amount)
- Buttons

SKILLS

- Sew a drop-shoulder sleeve
- Sew a patch pocket
- Apply fusible interfacing
- Sew neck and front facings

HOW TO SEW AN UNLINED JACKET

1 Prepare the fabric (page 25). Lay out the pattern pieces (page 32), and cut out (page 36) all but the facings. Fuse interfacing to the wrong side of the fabric for the facings, following the manufacturer's directions (p. 98). Then cut out the facings. Transfer any necessary marks (page 37).

(continued)

2 Turn under the top edge of the pocket ¼"
(6 mm); press. To finish the edge, set your
machine for a zigzag stitch of medium length and
width. Stitch close to the folded edge, so that the
right-hand swing of the needle just clears the fold.

3 Turn the upper edge of the pocket (the facing)
to the outside on the foldline; pin at the sides.
Starting at the top of the pocket, stitch a ⅝" (1.5 cm)
seam to the bottom of the facing on each side of the
pocket, backstitching at the beginning and end. Trim
the facing seam allowance to ⅜" (1 cm). Trim the
upper corners diagonally.

4 Turn the facing to the inside. Using a point
turner or similar tool, gently push out the corners to square them off. Press the top fold. If the
pocket has square bottom corners, turn under ⅝"
(1.5 cm) on the bottom, and press. Then repeat for
the side edges.

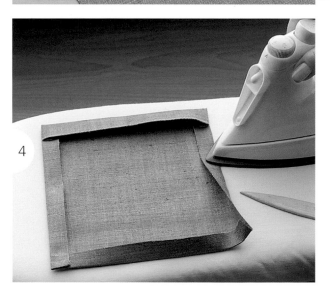

5 Set your sewing machine for a straight stitch of 10 to 12 stitches per inch, which is 2 to 2.5 mm. Measure the finished width of the facing; subtract ⅛" (3 mm). Mark this distance from the needle on the machine bed, using tape. Topstitch the upper edge of the pocket, guiding the fold along the tape mark and catching the facing in the stitches.

6 Repeat steps 2 to 5 for the other pocket. Place the pockets on the jacket front, matching the upper corners to the markings transferred from the pattern. Pin them securely in place, **inserting the pins perpendicular to the edges** (p. 43). Edgestitch around the sides and bottom of the pockets, backstitching at both upper corners. Stop with the needle down in the fabric to pivot at each corner. **Remove the pins as you come to them** (p. 43).

(continued)

7 Pin the jacket fronts to the jacket back at the shoulders, with right sides together, aligning the cut edges and matching any notches. Insert the pins perpendicular to the edges.

8 Stitch the seams, guiding the cut edges along the ⅝" (1.5 cm) seam allowance guide. Press the seams flat; then press them open.

9 Sew the front facings to the back facing at the shoulders as in steps 7 and 8. Trim the seam allowances to ¼" (6 mm). Finish the inner, unnotched edges of the front facings and the lower edge of the back facing (arrows) as in step 2.

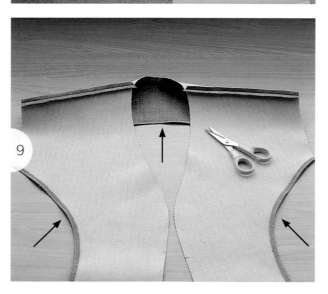

10 Pin the facing to the jacket, right sides together, aligning the cut edges. Match the shoulder seams and all notches. At the shoulders, insert a pin in the wells of the seams, to keep them aligned.

11 Stitch the facing to the jacket, guiding the cut edges along the ⅝" (1.5 cm) seam allowance guide. Stitch continuously from one lower edge, around the neckline, to the opposite lower edge; backstitch a few stitches at the beginning and end. Remove the pins as you come to them, and keep the shoulder seam allowances open flat.

12 Grade the seam allowances by trimming the jacket neckline seam allowance to ⅜" (1 cm) and the facing seam allowance to ¼" (6 mm). Clip into the neckline seam allowance every ½" (1.3 cm), clipping up to, but not through, the stitches. Clipping allows the facing to turn smoothly to the inside and lie flat.

(continued)

13 Press the seam allowances flat; then press them toward the facing. With the right side up, place the facing (A) under the presser foot, so the needle is aligned to enter the fabric just to the right of the seam at the lower left front; the jacket (B) extends off the left of the machine bed. Keeping the seam allowance turned toward the facing (arrows), stitch all around the fronts and neckline very close to the seam. You will be stitching through the facing and the seam allowance, but not through the jacket. This step, called understitching, helps the facing lie flat.

✂ **TIP** *Along the curve of the neckline, keep the facing lying flat, allowing the jacket to "bunch up" to the left of the curve. Stitch, following the curve of the facing. The clipped seam allowance will "fan out" underneath the facing.*

14 Turn the facing to the inside; press. Align the shoulder seams, and smooth them out to the sleeve edge. Pin the facing to the sleeve edge, inserting the pins perpendicular to the edge. Set your machine for long straight stitches. Baste the facings to the sleeve edges.

✂ **TIP** *Some jacket patterns have facings that do not extend all the way to the sleeve edge. Align the shoulder seam allowances, and **stitch in the ditch** (p. 85) to secure the facing to the jacket.*

15 Pin the sleeve to the jacket, with right sides together. Align the cut edges, and match the notches. You probably also have a mark on the sleeve edge that aligns to the jacket shoulder seam. Count the notches to be sure you are pinning the correct sleeve. Pin frequently from the jacket side, easing the sleeve to fit smoothly.

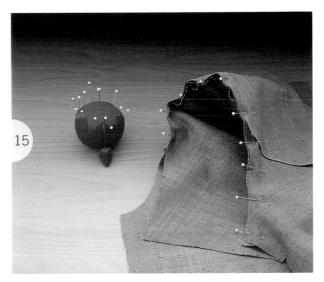

16 Place the jacket under the presser foot, with the sleeve underneath. Stitch the seam, guiding the edges along the ⅝" (1.5 cm) seam allowance guide. Remove the pins as you come to them.

17 Check from the sleeve side, to be sure there are no puckers. If there are any, clip the stitches, using a seam ripper, and remove the stitches on either side of the pucker far enough to smooth it out; restitch.

(continued)

18 Stitch a second line in the seam allowances, ¼" (6 mm) from the first stitching line, from the notches to each end. Trim the seam allowances in this area close to the second stitching line.

19 Repeat steps 15 to 18 for the opposite sleeve. Set your machine for a medium-length, medium-width zigzag stitch. For each sleeve, finish the seam allowance edges together, stitching so that the right swing of the needle just clears the fabric edge. Press the seam allowances toward the sleeves.

20 Pin the jacket front to the jacket back, right sides together, along the side seams and extending on to the underarm sleeve seams. Match notches, and align the sleeve seams. Insert the pins perpendicular to the edges.

21 Stitch ⅝" (1.5 cm) seam from the bottom of one side continuously to the end of the sleeve. Keep the underarm seam allowances turned toward the sleeve. Repeat for the opposite side.

22 Finish the side and underarm seam allowances as in step 2. Press the seam allowances flat; then press them open.

✂ **TIP** *Press the seam allowances open over a seam roll to prevent imprinting the seam allowance edges onto the right side of the jacket and to make it easier to press the sleeve seams open.*

(continued)

23 Finish the lower edge of the jacket as in step 2. Repeat for the lower edges of the sleeves. Turn under the remaining hem allowances on the sleeves, and press, using a seam roll or sleeve board (page 18). Slipstitch (page 52) the hems to the jacket.

24 Place the jacket on your ironing board, wrong side up; open the front facings. Turn under the remaining hem allowance on the lower edge, including the facings; press.

25 Unfold the lower edge. Turn the jacket over, and turn the facing to the outside, aligning the lower edges. Pin, keeping the facing seam allowances turned toward the facing. Stitch the facing to the jacket, stitching in the well of the pressed fold. Repeat for the opposite side.

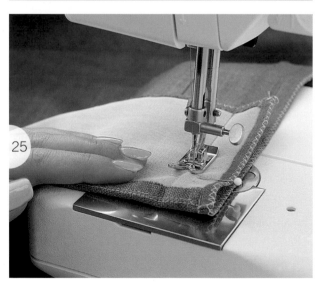

26 Trim the facing seam allowance to within ¼" (6 mm) of the stitches. Trim the corner diagonally, to within ⅛" (3 mm) of the corner stitch. Repeat for the opposite side. Turn the facings to the inside, and press.

27 Refold the remaining hem, and pin. Slipstitch the hem to the jacket. At the fronts, slipstitch the facings to the hem.

28 Topstitch ⅜" (1 cm) from the edges along the fronts and neckline of the jacket, if desired. If your jacket has buttons, transfer the buttonhole placement marks from your pattern to the right jacket front. Make buttonholes, following the directions in your sewing machine owner's manual. Transfer the button placement marks to the left front. Sew buttons as on page 50 or 51.

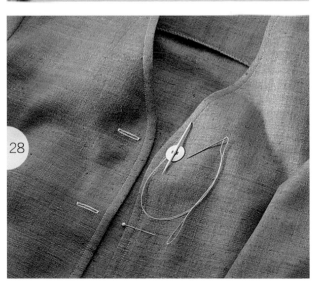

glossary

BACKSTITCHING. Taking a few backward stitches at the beginning and end of your stitching line prevents the stitches from pulling out. The method for backstitching varies with each sewing machine. You may need to lift and hold your stitch length lever, push in and hold a button, or simply touch an icon. Check your owner's manual.

BASTE. Long, easy-to-remove stitches are sewn into the fabric temporarily, either by hand or by machine. Hand-basting stitches are used to hold layers of fabric and batting together for quilting. Machine-basting stitches are used to close a seam before inserting a zipper. They are also used to gather a section of fabric into a smaller space.

BIAS. Any diagonal line intersecting the lengthwise and crosswise grains of fabric is referred to as bias. While woven fabric does not stretch on the lengthwise and crosswise grains, it has considerable stretch on the bias.

CASING. A fabric tunnel is sewn into the garment, often at the waistline, to carry elastic or cording.

CLIP. Small, closely spaced cuts are made into the seam allowances of a garment or other project, usually along a curve or into a corner. When the item is turned right side out, the seam allowances can spread apart and lie flat where they have been clipped. Small clips are also used for marking the location of notches or dots from the pattern.

COURSES. Corresponding to the crosswise grain of a woven fabric, the courses of a knit fabric run perpendicular to the selvages and ribs. Knit fabrics are most stretchy in the direction of the courses.

CROSSWISE GRAIN. On woven fabric, the crosswise grain runs perpendicular to the selvages. Fabric has slight "give" in the crosswise grain.

DROP LENGTH is the length of a tablecloth from the edge of the table to the edge of the cloth. It can be anywhere from 6" (15 cm) to floor-length.

DROP-SHOULDER. This garment design feature means that the seam joining the sleeve to the front and back is intended to fall down off the edge of the shoulder, rather than align to the shoulder crest. Drop-shoulder styles are relaxed, less fitted, and generally have more room in the armhole.

EASE refers to the amount of space built into a pattern beyond the actual body measurements.

EDGESTITCH. With the machine set for straight stitching at a length of 2 to 2.5 mm or 10 stitches per inch, stitch within ⅛" (3 mm) of a finished edge. With many machines, this can be achieved by guiding the inner edge of the right presser foot toe along the outer finished edge.

FACING. A fabric extension or addition that is sewn as a backing to another piece protects raw edges or seam allowances from raveling and gives the item a neat, finished appearance. For instance, a jacket front and neckline have an outer layer and an underlayer, or facing.

GATHER. Two rows of long machine stitches are sewn along a seamline. When the bobbin threads are pulled, the fabric slides along the threads into tiny tucks. Gathers are used to fit a wide garment section to a narrower section while at the same time adding shaping.

GRADING. Seam allowances on faced edges are trimmed to graduated widths to eliminate a bulky ridge. Often the garment seam allowance is trimmed to ¼" (6 mm) and the facing seam allowance is trimmed to ⅛" (3 mm).

HEMMING. The outer edge of a project is given a neat finished appearance by turning under and securing the raw edge in one of several methods.

LENGTHWISE GRAIN. On woven fabric, the lengthwise grain runs parallel to the selvages. Fabrics are generally stronger and more stable along the lengthwise grain.

MARK. It is often necessary to give yourself temporary guidelines or guide points on the fabric for cutting, stitching, or matching seams. There are many tools and methods for doing this, such as marking pencils and pens, chalk dispensers, tape, or pins.

MITER. Excess fabric is folded out at an angle to eliminate bulk. You probably miter the corners when you wrap gifts.

NAP. Some fabrics have definite up and down directions, either because of a surface pile, like corduroy or velveteen, or because of a one-way print. When laying out a pattern on napped fabric, cut all the pieces with the top edges facing the same direction.

NONDIRECTIONAL PRINT. The design printed on this fabric has no definite up and down directions, and pattern pieces can be laid out with the top edges facing in either direction.

PATCH POCKETS. One of the easiest pocket styles to sew, these are sewn to the outer surface of the garment like a patch.

PIVOT. Perfect corners are stitched by stopping with the needle down in the fabric at the exact corner before turning. To be sure the corner stitch locks, turn the handwheel until the needle goes all the way down and just begins to rise. Then raise the presser foot, turn the fabric, lower the presser foot, and continue stitching.

PRESHRINK. Fabric that shrinks, especially natural fibers, shrinks most in the first laundering. If you intend to launder your finished item occasionally, you should wash the fabric before cutting out the pieces, so the item will not shrink after you

make it. Dry clean only fabrics can be preshrunk by steaming them with your iron.

PRESS. This step is extremely important to the success of your sewing projects. Select the heat setting appropriate for your fabric, and use steam. Lift and lower the iron in an overlapping pattern. Do not slide the iron down the seam, as this can cause the fabric to stretch out of shape, especially on the crosswise grain or bias.

RIBBING is a very stretchy knit fabric, usually with pronounced ridges. It is especially suitable for necks and cuffs on knit garments, since it can easily stretch to go over heads and hands, yet spring back into shape once in place. Most ribbing comes in much narrower widths than other fabrics and, because you use less of it, it is often sold by the inch (centimeter) rather than the yard (meter).

RIBS. Corresponding to the lengthwise grain in woven fabric, the ribs of a knit fabric run parallel to the selvages (if there are any). Knits are usually most stable in the rib direction.

SEAM. Two pieces of fabric are placed right sides together and joined along the edge with stitches. After stitching, the raw edges are hidden on the wrong side, leaving a clean, smooth line on the right side.

SEAM ALLOWANCE. Narrow excess fabric lies between the

stitching line and the raw edges. The standard seam allowance width for woven-fabric garment sewing is ⅝" (1.5 cm); the standard width for knit-fabric garments is ¼" (6 mm); the standard width for home décor sewing is ½" (1.3 cm). The seam allowance gives the seam strength and ensures that the stitches cannot be pulled off the raw edges.

SEAM ALLOWANCE GUIDE. Most machines have a series of lines on the throat plate. These lines mark the distance from the needle (where a standard straight stitch seam would be) to the cut edges. Measure these lines on your machine to determine where the edge of your fabric should be for the width seam you are stitching.

SEAM RIPPER. It doesn't really rip. Use the sharp point to slide under and cut stitches one at a time. Avoid the temptation to simply slide the cutting hook down the seam. You will inevitably cut into your fabric. Even the most experienced sewers rely on their seam rippers.

SELVAGES. Characteristic of woven fabrics, this narrow, tightly woven outer edge should be cut away. Avoid the temptation to use it as one side of a cut piece, as it may cause the seam to pucker and may shrink excessively when laundered.

TACKING. Short stationary stitches, sewn by hand or by machine, hold two or more pieces of fabric together a little less conspicuously then a row of stitches.

index

THREAD JAM. The threads become tangled up in a wad on the underside of the fabric and the machine gets stuck. The best way to prevent a thread jam is to hold both top and bottom thread tails to the back or side of the presser foot until completing the first few stitches of a seam. If a thread jam happens, DON'T USE FORCE! Remove the presser foot, if you can. Snip all the threads you can get at from the top of the throat plate. Open the bobbin case door or throat plate, and snip any threads you can get at. Remove the bobbin, if you can. Gently remove the fabric. Thoroughly clean out the feed dog and bobbin area before reinserting the bobbin and starting over.

TOPSTITCHING is a decorative and functional stitching line placed ¼" to 1" (6 mm to 2.5 cm) from the finished edge of an item. The stitching is done with the right side of the item facing up. Sometimes topstitching is done with a heavier thread or two threads through the machine needle, to make it more visible.

UNDERSTITCHING is straight stitching very close to the seamline that connects a facing to the garment, and it keeps the facing from rolling to the outside of the garment. After the seam allowances are trimmed, clipped, and pressed toward the facing, stitch from the right side of the facing.

MORE BOOKS ON SEWING

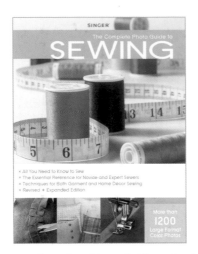

The Complete Photo Guide to Sewing
Editors of Creative Publishing
ISBN: 978-1-58923-434-5

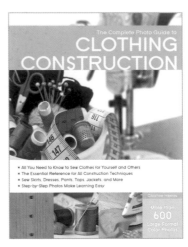

The Complete Photo Guide to Clothing Construction
Christine Haynes
ISBN: 978-1-58923-777-3

Sewing Clothes Kids Love
Nancy Langdon and Sabine Pollehn
ISBN: 978-1-58923-473-4

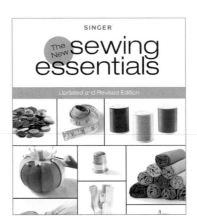

SINGER: The New Sewing Essentials
Editors of Creative Publishing
ISBN: 978-1-58923-432-1